Scot Lit Ann

DB8730

£14

First published by The Word Bank in 2015.
Registered Office:
8 Jackson's Entry, Edinburgh EH8 8PJ

Copyright: The Contributors
This book is sold subject to the condition that it shall not, by way of trade or otherwise, be lent, resold, hired out, or otherwise circulated without the publisher's prior consent in any form of binding or cover other than that in which it is published and without a similar condition including this condition being imposed on the subsequent publisher.

All rights reserved. No part of this publication may be reproduced, stored in a retrieval system or transmitted in any form or by any means, electronic, mechanical or otherwise without the written permission of the publisher.

Design:
a visual agency | avisualagency.com
with Kat Loudon, assisted by Ellen Macdonald.
Thanks to Edwin Pickstone at The Press.

Printing:
Bell & Bain Ltd, Glasgow and DCI Print Management

A catalogue record of this book is available from the British Library. 9780993054419
ISBN : 978-0-9930544-1-9 | £15

THE EVERGREEN

◆◆◆◆◆◆◆◆◆◆◆◆◆◆◆◆◆◆

A NEW SEASON IN THE NORTH

CONTENTS

10	Introduction	Sean Bradley
13	The Festival Director	Peter Burnett
23	Lucky Spence's Last Advice Part II	Petra Reid
29	Development	Robert Davies
41	What if the City Fails to Work	Ali Millar
51	Sonnets to Robert Fergusson	David Wheatley
61	Shop Girls of Edinburgh	Lucy Ellmann
		Illustrations by Diana Hope
71	The Abolition of the University	Lou Dear
81	Street Music	Jim Gilchrist
91	Untethered	James Kelman
97	Folk, Work, Film	Kenny Munro
107	Adventures in Austeritania	Eddie Gibbons
111	A World in Action	Elizabeth Darling
125	Latticing, Hexagons and Enchanters	Tom Hubbard
135	Outside: Inside	Paul Furneaux
147	Letter from Barcelona	Brian McLaughlin
158	Floodlands of the Duckabush	Ken Crump
160	Footfall, or Death of Tourist	Joyce Guthrie
161	The Lock Up 1969	Neil Young
163	The Pocketbook Guide to Scottish Superheroes	Kirsti Wishart
172	The Burry Man	Diana Hope
173	Contributor Biographies	

Editorial Board:
Sean Bradley, Elizabeth Elliott, Andrew Guest, Edward Hollis, Todd McEwen

The Word Bank is a community publishing collective run by Edinburgh Old Town Development Trust.

Edinburgh Old Town Development Trust is a Scottish charity (SC042964) committed to the revitalisation of the Old Town through stimulating growth in community participation, the arts and enterprise. It aims to support a vibrant, sustainable community in the Old Town by developing enterprising projects to meet local needs; establishing a network of gardens and green spaces; promoting education and training; and preserving the area's built and cultural heritage.

Acknowledgements:
Supported by Creative Scotland, Saltire Society Scotland and Edinburgh World Heritage Trust.

ALBA | CHRUTHACHAIL

EDINBURGH WORLD HERITAGE

INTRODUCTION

WHAT WE ARE COMING TO IS... INDUSTRY ENNOBLED BY EDUCATION

PATRICK GEDDES
1891

The view from the City Chambers down the High Street suggests that the transformation of Edinburgh from an industrial city – a description the city fathers have always been reluctant to acknowledge – is now complete. Across the street, the figure of Adam Smith, the so-called prophet of Thatcherism, stands with his back not only to the Castle but also to the traditional professions of the capital: the law, the church, local government and culture (the National Library, if you will). His gaze is towards the Canongate where no longer gasworks, printing works or brewery can be found, their stench replaced, as reported in the first volume of this journal, by the pervasive aromas of coffee and leisure.

The new work of the city and its people is servicing visitors like so many invisible hands; visitors who wish to partake of Edinburgh, its glory and gore, its learning in science, philosophy and literature, and the tartan shreds of a fabricated culture everywhere draped at greatly reduced prices the length of the Mile. If they follow Adam Smith's gaze, nowhere can the visitor see the population working for itself; it has no time to bake its own bread or put out fresh fruit and vegetables, fish or meat for its sustenance. Indeed the visitors may wonder if anyone lives here at all. After all, how could they?

The Evergreen seeks to remind us that successful and sustainable communities have three essential elements in balance: environment, economy and society. How to produce, in a global society, a mixed economy balancing, in Geddes's terms, Place, Work, and Folk is now the major challenge. Adam Smith, whichever way you think he is facing, was sufficiently sceptical of the workings of commercial interests to encourage our city councillors, however strapped for cash they are, to scrutinise what it is they think they are offering. To strive towards a long-term vision for the city and not seek short term gains.

In the Old Town we have ample opportunity to learn, to debate and remake the city we want. The university, its teachers and students are everywhere evident. Patrick Geddes was not alone in seeing the university as essential to the success of this place and its inhabitants, contributing knowledge and skills to the betterment of Edinburgh's people and economy. That's as good a starting point for urban renewal as any.

Sean Bradley, Editor
September 2015

THE FESTIVAL DIRECTOR

◆◆◆◆◆◆◆◆◆◆◆◆◆◆◆◆◆

PETER BURNETT

It was a bright spring day in Scotland – perfect conditions for agriculture but lousy for the dwellers of the city. A robust wind blew me along the pavement to my meeting, past doorways in which heads that had long ago divested themselves of any sex-appeal were trying to light cigarettes. By mid-morning, everyone who had somewhere to go was already there, leaving only a few drifters like myself and the looming cavities of empty buses as they tried the hills. I got to The Filmhouse early and bought a coffee and I was logging my phone on to their wireless when Alison Cutlette moved sedately into the room.

I'd known Cutlette for years but she had never called me for a meeting like this. I was intrigued. Arts administration in Edinburgh is a crook's paradise. Budgets are large and salaries are prodigious, the lunches are monumental and the holidays are whopping, the parties are extensive and the adjectives are cyclopean, and best of all there's very little work to do. Generally, if you work for one of Edinburgh's many festivals all that is required of you is one month of heavy socialising, followed by a month's holiday and then ten months of bathing in the glory of the reputations of other people. Pacified by the quaint desires of your board of directors, you commission artists to come up with schemes to support arts that were thriving before you got there and the rest of the time is spent on social media, with your days punctuated by functions and the enormous satisfaction of knowing that you are better paid and more respected than any of the artists you patronise.

Alison Cutlette was with her PA, whom she kissed and dismissed. Then she gave me that 'delighted to see you smile' that is quintessentially 'arts admin' and weaved over the room, sitting down and opening her diary at today's date. Other than the doodles and the mention of my name (followed by a question mark – what was that all about?) the page was relatively empty. Page-a-day paper diaries have always been optimistic but in arts admin it's worse and if it weren't for the doodles your life would be nothing but one long unregulated coffee break.

Cutlette and I looked at the empty page:
PETER BURNETT?

'How are you doing Peter?' asked Cutlette.

The PA was at the bar, purchasing a coffee for her boss.

'I'm fine,' I said. Had I had it in me to include the repellent whole of my day, I would not have said that I was fine but I doubt that Cutlette would have enjoyed that, so feigning it seemed wise. But I was not fine. I was unemployed again, and my book was on the rack.

'How is the Jean-Luc Godard book coming along?' she asked next.

'It's OK,' I lied. 'It's hard with a young kid – but guess what? We're due our next baby in three weeks. So I don't know if I'll get the book finished any time soon.'

'Congratulations,' said Cutlette, a shiver in her womb. 'I read on your blog that you wanted the book finished by Christmas – but that was three months ago, wasn't it?'

'I'm afraid so,' I said.

('Damn my blog,' I thought.)

Alison Cutlette's PA arrived with the great woman's coffee and Cutlette stirred in the milk. I watched this, thinking of those great cup-a-coffee shots from Godard's Vivre Sa Vie and 2 or 3 Things I Know About Her.

'Peter,' said Cutlette slowly, 'I have a favour to ask.'

'Of course,' I said, and I smiled with the emphatic politeness of somebody who would really like a job, any job.

'As you might know we are showing an excerpt of Godard's latest film at the Film Festival,' she said. 'It's by special arrangement with Office Fédéral de la Culture.'

I nodded. I liked the way she said that. It was amusing that while she didn't speak French, Cutlette was able to stress the pronunciation into something that sounded authentic, but wasn't. Of course I'm being uncharitable. Alison Cutlette gave the French a good go but it was hideously funny, almost impossible to reproduce.

'Well Godard is coming,' she said.

Now that was news. In this land-of-no-surprises it was good to hear this sort of thing from time to time.

'That's great,' I said. 'What would you like me to do?'

'Godard is coming next week,' said Alison Cutlette and from her bowed head, I could tell she didn't think that it was great news at all. In fact, the way that she looked at her coffee, it was all gloom. Perhaps Cutlette had heard tell of Godard's belief that cinema was dead. Perhaps she had sensed Godard's deep loathing for people like herself who made a living by namedropping their way from snack to tea. I waited.

'Yes,' she said. 'Godard is coming to Edinburgh and he wants to show a video and we agreed, although we don't know what we've agreed to. Certainly he's welcome. He's one of the world's greatest living directors.'

'Very interesting,' I said.

So we all knew that Godard was one of the world's greatest living directors, because we all had the internet. But what could Cutlette add to that?

She was staring into her coffee and I thought again about the oddity of Godard having anything to do with her – with us. Godard wasn't on Twitter so little wonder she couldn't understand him.

'Thing is,' said Cutlette. 'We thought you may be the person to go to the airport and pick up Godard. He doesn't want a taxi and he doesn't want to go to his hotel. He wants one of us to come for him so for the duration you are going to be Edinburgh Film Festival staff. How does that sound?'

'It sounds all right,' I said. Cutlette poked her cake with a spoon as if the unpronounceable emulsifying agents within it had depressed her into quiescence. 'Why me?'

The question was fair. There were others I could name whose salaries would have included their partaking of adventures such as this, and even if they hadn't wanted to, there were more who were higher on the pecking order than myself when it came to such privilege.

'Why didn't you ask Franklin Marsh?' I added. As Edinburgh's best known film reviewer, Marsh seemed the natural choice.

'We did ask Franklin,' said Cutlette, 'only he doesn't speak French and you do. Between you and me, Franklin hasn't seen many of Godard's films. He's trying to catch up now but it isn't really his thing. He likes most French directors but Godard leaves him cold.'

'Well Godard is Swiss and not French,' I said – a statement which caused Cutlette to gasp.

'You're kidding?' she said. With her mouth open she looked like a frightened horse. 'You are absolutely kidding?' she asked.

As soon as I said 'No,' Cutlette scrambled for her phone and began a text. I sat back and watched while this proceeded. The text was followed by two emails.

'I'm sorry,' said Cutlette as she typed. 'This doesn't look good. I've written two press releases this morning and fifteen fucking tweets'.

Alison Cutlette waved frantically towards the door of the Filmhouse bar. There was the PA.

'Godard – is – Swiss'.

Cutlette mouthed the words without sounding them but the PA had no hope of comprehension. She shook her head and Alison Cutlette whispered the words this time, although the PA remained confused, red faced, pretty, but in essence out of her depth.

'Go get a fish?' mouthed the PA in return. Glassy-eyed, she was at a loss. PAs in Edinburgh are used to the most finical requests. It happens all the time that they are asked to fetch some fish and complain about the quality of cocktail cherries.

'You can easily say Godard is French', I said. 'He was born in Paris but his father's Swiss and he was brought up in Switzerland – and I think you'll find he holds a Swiss passport'.

'He's Swiss!' shouted Cutlette, loud enough to be heard by her PA and many others. Loud enough, but not clear enough, and so the PA was bid approach. It was only when she neared us that the PA received her text message from Alison Cutlette, read it, turned a further hue of crimson and ran from the bar. In running the PA resembled a wounded wading bird, her legs forced by her skirt into an unnatural twist.

'Good God', said Cutlette. 'I'm glad I called you now. You see Peter this is a good sign. A good thing that we called you'.

We were being watched by the round faces of the many early lunchers in the Filmhouse bar. People take this sort of excitement seriously in Edinburgh. If anybody raises their voice at lunch in Edinburgh you can tell that a cultural disaster is near. Alison Cutlette wrote GODARD IS A SWISS in her diary and circled it, then she stared at the statement as if she could make it last forever.

'I would have gone to pick Godard up myself,' she whispered, and even glanced around the bar in case her confession was picked up. 'I just haven't seen any Godard. Has anyone?'

'They don't show them on television,' I said, 'but the enthusiast can always find the basics on DVD'.

'I saw Alphaville and Le Weekend,' she said, 'but I don't remember much about either one.'

'It's just called Weekend', I said, as nicely as I could, but of course I regretted it. Correcting people more than once a day isn't a good way to make friends in the arts.

'We asked at the university', she went on. 'Someone is doing a paper on Godard but they don't speak French and the person that does speak French can't do it. There were postgrads who could speak French and were willing to go and some of them had seen a few Godard films.'

Alison Cutlette turned the pages of her diary until she found the list. The page was scored with markings, phone numbers and doodles, there must have been fifteen names there. She ran her pen down the page.

'Nightmare', she said. 'None of them were any good. And these ones didn't respond'.

The pen hovered on one person's name and then drifted at a curious angle to the next.

'This is the one I wanted. She said she would do it and then she vanished. And this guy was going to do it but he changed his mind at the last minute.'

She turned the page. Another set of scored-out individuals. Probably ten. I spotted my name. It was circled but not scored out.

'I begged Franklin but he wouldn't touch it. Godard won't speak English. He just won't apparently.'

'It's an ideological thing,' I said. 'English is the language America uses to dominate world cinema with its genre based attacks on the art form.'

'Really?' asked Cutlette. She'd stopped to calculate the implications of my last statement. 'I wonder how he feels about Scotland?' she asked.

'I'll be happy to meet him and bring him in from the airport,' I said.

I smiled, and was pleased. The thought of meeting Godard was rightly exciting me and to have come at least fortieth in their list of candidates was a compliment I was not going to ignore.

'Very good,' said Cutlette, and the job was done. 'I'll email you details. Godard doesn't want to go to his hotel so I thought you could take him to our office. We'll have a translator. Godard has an interview with Franklin when he gets here so you'll have to hand him over to us promptly. Then we're showing the Godard video but there aren't any seats left for that.'

Cutlette began the complicated routine of confirming all of this in her diary, again writing my name, and drawing a large rectangle which remained empty. Perhaps that would be where my final score would go?

'When we sat down,' I said, 'you asked if I would do you a favour.'

Cutlette looked up, fleet of face. Then she surveyed me calmly.

'This isn't a job then?' I asked.

Alison Cutlette sighed and turned her pen around on the page. She knew what I was thinking – where I would park my car for all of this and would I get petrol expenses? The Film Festival office was in the city's indeterminate no-parking-on-pain-of-imprisonment zone, so I'd either be getting traffic tickets or shepherding Godard in and out of a taxi that I would have to pay for. I hated to ask about payment because I knew they never stumped up for writers. There's money for badges and back supports, and there's always tens of thousands for rebranding and for the consultation fees necessary to choose the correct designer pink rocking chair. There's money for marketing campaigns and for the development of apps and there's money for courses on how to use Facebook, but try being a writer in their midst and see if they'll pay you – because they won't. Cutlette was even being paid to have this meeting with me but I was the one losing valuable writing time. I was the one taking the morning off to shepherd Godard into Edinburgh and I was expected to do it for free, because I was a writer. Alison Cutlette would put the cake she wasn't eating on expenses and yet I was the one being made to feel like a dick for requesting disbursement. The Film Festival had never done anything to help me and had in fact never replied to a single email I had written them. It's another of the great benefits of working in arts admin – you never reply to emails. You just let 'em build up and delete them all as junk.

'There isn't a budget for this,' said Alison Cutlette, rather harshly I thought. But on the day that the fates had ended my journalistic career for good and in light of the publisher's threats to recoup their advance from me, I had been stupid to ask for money.

'Yeah I guess,' I said.

Alison Cutlette pushed away her cake in a manner which reminded me of my family's inability to finish their own food.

'I can't conceive of eating this,' she said.

I glanced at the sponge. Why do we remind our children of the hungry people in the world but never treat adults to this humiliation? What would they do with a slice of chocolate chip angel cake in sub-Saharan Africa, anyway?

Alison Cutlette gathered her papers.

'I have a meeting,' she said. Of course she had a meeting – that was all she did. She was in a meeting with me, presumably? I was a meeting, wasn't I? Why do they always say they have a meeting when they are in a meeting? The world is skew whiff. It's artists and writers that are working to create the arts that they are supposed to be administering and it's them that are paid. It's them that are justifying everything by being in meetings, but it's not a life. It's a parasitical attack on the defenceless handicrafters of culture.

'Phone me when you've got Godard,' said the Cutlette. 'Deliver him to the Film Festival office but hand him over downstairs.'

As we walked from the Filmhouse bar, Cutlette said hello to a few people and then an apparatus tactfully bleeped in her pocket and she glided away. This meeting was over and I had received my commission. Presently came a stupendous laugh from the stairs as Alison Cutlette bumped into someone she hadn't seen for a while and they kissed. I watched their shouts and gestures and then dragged myself on to the street. The whole morning had passed and I had done no work to speak of. If I wasn't to be paid, I wanted something out of this – but what?

LUCKY SPENCE'S LAST ADVICE PART II

◆·•·•·◆·•·•·◆·•·•·◆·•·•·◆·•·•·◆·•·•·◆·•·•·◆·•·•·◆

PETRA REID

To South Bridge! And the sale of things
Under a Kirk that lost both wings,
Where hens meet stags, sweet queens and kings
            In drunk parade;
From a bench our wee madam sings
            Her last tirade.

All you joke Jacobite laddies,
You ghost faking haggis caddies
Spieling tales like Cowgate haddies,
            Let me narrate
Some facts re dear local gadgies –
            As of this date.

I'll give you The Real Reekie Tour,
Backsides broadsides I'm all sides poor:
Spare some change for a Hunter (Square) hoor?
            (As such forbye
Outwith Social Help Care or Cure)
            Caught your eye, ken.

For Sparte and Edina's low
Skinny grande cappuccino
Cup's a begging bowl that's bio-
            Degradable
Earning more than a quickie blow
            (Debateable).

Thriving on chips'n'coke Big Mac:
Come dinnertime I've done my whack –
This zero job avoids the sack,
            And broo sanctions:
Lunching ladies - get off my back!
            Where's your husbands?

Observe the Grecian symmetries
Of me outside your hostelries –
A blanket's classic draperies
                O'er crossed legs,
Hens and stags play joke raperies,
                Fuck you! Tron dregs.

Dodging Old and New Town radar
I'm not hi-viz like your builder
Pouring foundations for mergers
                And investment;
My body's capital ventures
                Command low rent.

I don't want to be a downer –
But how long for Blair Street's last sauna
Since big Polis Scotland's grown a
                Wee Free conscience?
Spare some change (On the streets with her!)
                Or tolerance?

Lap dancing legal podiums
Just delay street sex odiums
('Girls on the game – let's discount them,
                Know what we mean?
Nae heels nae hair nae home quorums –
                They don't do clean!')

Junkie smackheid bitch: en retard
Auld alliances marked my card
I was nee known comme wee bastard
                Ne'er do well,
I'll rive your brats, kick your doup hard
                And play the Deel.

All you Lords' Acts of Sederunt
Safeguarding property – they're cant
To a common green miscreant
              And civic fail,
I decree posh Edina burnt
                  Down in detail.

I knew a skank (this is no shite)
To spontaneously ignite
On Costas terrace – dead, all right?
                    How's that for cruel?
God Save Our World Heritage Site
                  From lighter fuel.

You might say conservation laws
Keep pillars for us ancient bawds
Who dance like leaves round privy lords
                  In rank commerce;
You keep whistling whiles ane, whiles twa,
                  Maister Geddes.

30p a pee's council sense -
But punters inconvenience:
I'll rent them no deep clean and cleansed
                    Germ free spunk box.
Still, I'll not die in douce silence –
                  Jingling coins talk.

Camera Obscura's what I blame,
Au revoir original shame –
Spying me tits up on The Game
                  Genes extanted:
The last corpus Athenian
                You guys wanted.

Dropped a bairn hidden on my own
Under Flodden Wall, born like stone.
Will Patrick's garden yet be sown
                In remembrance
For these Old Town flowers girls have borne
                Still with no chance?

You have a good bonsoir! Makes sense
When you're rich in legacy tense
And accept international pence –
                How free's my will?!
I'm no dead yet I'm Lucky Spence –
                Here for you, still.

DEVELOPMENT

ROBERT DAVIES

29

'Cities are the privilege scenes of memory, topographies in which the images of the unconscious of a culture corresponds with the memory of traces of the individual.'
– Ingeborg Bachmann

Ideas of memory linked to a place that will over time see its landscape alter have been key to this work. I set out to record the changing coastline of a city, and found a landscape in limbo, of stalled developments that had little connection to history and community – a landscape of unfinished visions of its future.

   I have an affinity with coastal places and communities, having grown up on the South Wales coast and lived in St Ives. Both places have witnessed changes brought on by development and the shifting needs of society – from the days when coal was exported around the world from Wales, to St Ives' transformation from a fishing port to a tourist resort. In Development I explore how ideas and experience of place change over time. The landscape we live in today is often completely different from how it used to be, and with the continuum of 'development', will become different again in the future.

   I wanted to find a location for my work that was undergoing change, somewhere that had a resonant history, evidence of which was being altered and perhaps lost in a new landscape. Edinburgh's coastline – the historic port communities of Granton, Newhaven, and Leith – is the location for the work in Development. These ports have been a conduit of history, once thriving communities of multicultural diversity even before the term was coined. Since 2000, developments have taken place in an attempt to give new life to these declining areas. These are now under the Forth Ports Master Plan to create a 'coastal quarter', with a mixture of retail units and luxury housing.

   After the Second World War 'reconstruction', as it was then termed, was key to rebuilding Britain's civilian housing. The decline of heavy industries such as mining and shipbuilding left communities without the very reasons for their existence. Industrial sites were abandoned; large areas of cities and towns became wasteland. A second wave of reconstruction began in the 1980s, when emerging financial wealth was created from new technology and the political embracing of the free market. It was during this period that the term 'regeneration' came to the fore. In his seminal paper, Urban 'regeneration': reflections on a metaphor (Sheffield Hallam University, 1999), Dr Robert Furby discusses how regeneration developments are sold by the use of aspirational and 'inspirational' language and ideologies. Redevelopment of Edinburgh's coast is entitled 'The Master Plan', the kind of terminology Furby likens to something carried out by a benevolent developer whose sole aim is to improve communities, motivated by the public good rather than private gain.

I am interested in the visual impact of these projects in Edinburgh, how their new 'community' spaces and housing seem to lack the key elements needed for community participation – opportunities for people to meet or engage with one another. The spaces in and around the developments have a sense of enclosure that acts to cut off, shut in and isolate. They could be viewed as compounds, wastelands, or office blocks, not a place designed to be a 'luxury urban village', or 'A place where people and their children want to live, work and play...'

Regeneration, according to Furby, is a word 'infused with religious hope' – the Latin translation of regeneration meaning new birth. The ideologies behind 're-birth' of urban wastelands, he notes, shifted during the 1980s from being institution- and government-led to being created by the new enterprise culture, which saw a profit to be made from the land, and by the societal shift to a new desire for home ownership. However, this move toward regeneration did not prevent, Furby notes, the continuing deterioration of many urban areas.

Construction began on the sites photographed in Development at the start of the millennium. Lack of financial and political cohesion has left them unfinished and falling into disrepair – producing a landscape of communities that sit disjointed and isolated from the city and its sense of place and history. Their temporary structures and safety barriers give off an ambiguity; without connection to place, they could be from a number of locations in the world, places perceived as dangerous or as utilitarian social housing, not the exclusive coastal communities of the developers' promises.

My focus on urban landscape has been influenced by the topographical photography of Bernd and Hilla Becher, and by American photographer Dan Graham and his 'Homes for America' essay, whose theme was housing projects of the 1960s. Robert Smithson's ideas in 'Hotel Palenque', which playfully investigated ideas around construction, time and history have also been influential. The work of painter George Shaw, who uses urban locations that suggest to the viewer a landscape devoid of human presence also had elements that I found visually resonant with the landscapes I encountered.

In Development I wanted to capture locations that might be familiar, although with an absence of the communities they were designed for. By recording them at particular moments, at different times of day, they are imbued with a desolate beauty. If "cities are the privilege scenes of memory" perhaps what was imagined for our collective memory of these places, and what has turned out to be the reality, are quite different things.

WHAT IF THE CITY FAILS TO WORK

ALI MILLAR

My city is a fiction.

Dreamt up first by my mother who studied here, and when we came up from the country – to break the monotony of the pastoral, the cows and the grass and the blue neon lit chip shop that was the only place to hang out; she would talk of the Cowgate, the Meadows, the no go areas for nice girls like her – like me.

But the city alters, shifts, areas change their own stories as planners, developers and residents reshape them until the city I know does not fit her narrative. I walk the meadows daily – my children play there. The Cowgate, well lit and over policed on a Saturday night and into the long mornings, does not scare me. This city works to hide its poor now, increasingly gentrified, made up, poverty pushed further and further to the periphery.

The city works.

The city seems to work.

The city takes on an identity of its own. It is bigger than me, exists before me and will, after me. The buildings do not need me, its reputation does not need me, I call it home, but do not dent it. It is a beast, bigger than the sum of its parts; it asserts its superiority and, in doing so, reaffirms my temporality.

This fear I have of the tenuous nature of being has only intensified since the birth of my children. I do not like to think of the long series of historical accidents that have led to me being me. People like to pin the existence of an ordered universe on God, to use it as evidence of a God. Only, it's not ordered at all, it's accident after accident after accident, only ever a building on things past.

As too is this existence of mine, it's just a big mistake. So many variables colliding, combining to result in me; my Grandparents' fortuitous escape from Poland, my Father's propensity for philandering, my Mother's vulnerability, and on it goes; it is reducible to that night, that position, that desire. I am only a combination of others' actions; until suddenly there I am, birthed, blue and unable to breathe. Here I am now, with the accident of self, and my husband's self and our accidents of children, living in a city, half planned, but still accidental. Only, we want so badly to believe otherwise. We call ourselves grown up, to remove our older self from the chaotic nature of childhood, to create some semblance of order, of intent.

But, it's fragile.

As are the webs we weave, for ourselves, to support ourselves, to support us, the citizens of this city. We call it infrastructure in an attempt to make it seem solid, strong, a structure strong enough to support us.

But it too is fragile.

Does the city work? Or is it, as is, an outdated concept?

What if it breaks and all this structure becomes too tenuous, not enough planning combining with too many accidents moving towards the inevitable point of crash, because crash we will; boom, bust, swings, roundabouts, Adam and Eve, Utopian Distopias – it's coming, so they say. But the point of breaking, we see, necessarily, as a future event. To contemplate otherwise is too terrible – too demanding. It means too much to see it in the present tense.

I know, we know, soon we will have to change, to ease our reliance on fossil fuels, on imported food, on capitalism, on scarce resources. Soon we must formulate a new way of living. But not now, not yet the petulant brat in me wails, not yet, leave it for my children, for their children. Let me have the easy option, the comfortable life; do not demand this change of me. But, change I must. Change we must. I do not want to work at it. I do not want to work hard at it.

What if it breaks? Tomorrow, soon, what if the uncomfortable is forced upon us? What if the city ceases to work for us?

In the book I'm reading the earth plunges rapidly towards a descent. It is the last days as predicted by the gospels, with shades of Revelation. There is an earthquake in the East Midlands, cutting off food supplies, shop shelves are bare, and a pregnant character begins to miss chocolate the most. It is the little things.

It is so fragile, this fiction we have built for ourselves, our cocooning comfort blankets of dairy, sugar and fat. It will not sustain us.

It's fiction, I tell myself.

It is, and yet.

Today, in the sun, the city works. Everything works better when it's like this. Near the Geddes gardens tourists sit in the Grassmarket, drink beer yards away from where once public hangings were entertainment, death a spectacle. Or so says a guide atop a boulder, Australian, his guidees American. We are a nation of storytellers, it is said, we made this nation up. We hide our dead now, ferry them in private ambulances to the city morgue, the Cowgate the Styx – but we parade and sell the historical, the fictive, dead; it's all Burke and Hare, Rebus and Rankin, tartan shops piping music into the street. It's what we trade in, this lie of nationhood, of unity, of a better past, but it brings in the tourists, and develops the city economically. That's the buzz word now, economic development, how the worth of proposed schemes is judged, it's a market driven economy, just as well we have something to sell. The city works, puts its past to work.

The city thrives on this uncomfortable co-dependency.

Stags leer as they eschew the pavement, walk towards the Cowgate, an arterial route, the vein of the city where once cattle were driven from country to city, to be sold in the Grassmarket. Now, where the two roads meet there's a community foodbank, asking online for donations of tinned pudding, packeted custard, this will feed empty stomachs, a quick fix, a temporary solution that does not educate as to how to cook economically. It's that word again, here the economic development falls down, will not feed the demonised poor the con-demnatory government sanction, use as pawns in an election year.

The city cracks.

The city works for some, but not for all, where does the tipping point sit, who calibrates the scales?

I walk the Cowgate, signalling my near past, the distant past, echoes, ghosts. The aptly named Underbelly venue is closed, out of season, not fit to entertain, instead it stores books, paper on paper of paper, where the smell lingers, tainting live acts with source coding. Books gather dust whilst women's refuges have none. UNESCO say we are a city of literature, a profitable designation.

The past might hover, but the present presses, as stags stagger, splutter, wolf whistle and spit. In The Three Sisters' garden of beer oversized screens turn overpaid demi-gods goliath sized for the stags to ape and to admire. Here in the city's bowels trapped tourists are hens, plastic penises mock bridal veils. Chekov turns, cannot rest.

Coffers swell, if this is development I don't want it. If this feeds the city does it feed me too?

The city works, just about.

A Tesco truck trundles by, headed no doubt to Holyrood, where until recently the nation's newspaper was printed; The Scotsman, reflective no longer – if ever – of many Scots men. To parliament, a dead man's folly where the leaders assemble, where SNP propose a national government – this will not end well. To Tesco, to restock shelves of a multinational corporation on the wane, no longer monopolising, mega stores downsizing, restructuring – a handy euphemism for cuts, but still, government subsidised, whilst the villainous poor, starve, do their own dental work.

Cracks, schisms – don't dare start looking, once seen you'll see them everywhere.

This country does not work.

In times of siege they used to wall the city up. Of plague close the city's gates. Starve the residents, the hungry will not revolt. What would happen then if besieged, by nature, by plague, by strikes, by fragility? It's all so fragile. It's all too fragile.

It will not break, not yet. Not now. The world is stable. The city endures. The world is not an accident. Say it often enough, you might be able to fool yourself.

By earlier logic, if I am accidental, if I so nearly was not, another day, another month, another man, another womb; and so by extension, all others too, then this stability is accidental, incidental, a flaw – a fiction.

How then to order it better, to make something we can stand up in, that endures, allows the city and us to endure. It's food, this politicising weapon, this old weapon of mine.

To backtrack and reveal, I have spent many years trying not to think about food, after too many years thinking only of food. I had a misspent youth, a wasted youth, where flesh atrophied, where I battled with myself to see how little I could weigh, how light I I could be and yet still stand up. Every day was a competition, a game of numbers, of checks and balances. And it was fun, so very much fun to begin with, when it blotted out that which it was meant to. But it quickly lost its gloss and I found myself trapped in this war of attrition against the self. For a while it looked like the only way out was the certain one, I was besieged by this illness, this thing Anorexia is. It was a beast of its own, I lived inside it, and yet, it was not of me, it was not me. It was saying something I was too scared to say, it was a profound statement I was making, just one I failed to understand, and one those around me failed too to understand, since it became only about food.

As if food is ever that simple.

During years of recovery food remained some kind of pharmakon to me, every mouthful holding within itself the possibility of poison and cure, fat or thin, to win or lose. After so many years of considering everything I put into my body, it was too much complexity, it got in the way; and instead of recovering fully, I recovered enough, through avoidance, by equating food to fuel, and leaving it at that. I did not want to ask or to know where it came from. It was just something to put in my mouth, to get me through the day, to chew quickly, and be done. But it bred ignorance in me, until now I cannot remember what seasons are for, what food grows when, or where, or how.

Tesco will not help me with that. My tummy rumbles, demands to be filled. I walk past the morgue with drunks drinking on the steps, crossroads where opposite, as a nearly not child I stood and pressed the button for the green man, excited to be here in the city, cold biting my fingers, blue eye shadow and liner, hair mascara, mistaking the smell of hops for baked potatoes. I miss the hops, I miss thinking it was potatoes, I miss potatoes, fresh from the ground, the feel of earth, the smell of the damp tubers, I miss my Grandpa, I miss home, I miss making home, I miss knowing how to live, how to do the things needed to sustain a life. This city does not work, for me. For me, this city does not work.

And yet, it's never just food. And never just about food.

I did not know how to feed myself. I stopped knowing because the complexity was too much to handle. And now, the city does not know how to feed itself, that much is evident. Again, the complexity is too much. Economic development is all well and good, but webs are fragile and tangled, the world spins, it might snap, and tourists then will not feed us unless we resort to desperate measures. We need to know as a city, which is little more than a collection of its citizens – how to nourish ourselves again. And Tesco will not help us.

Spinning, my head is light. I am light headed, as if without food my brain weighs less, does less. I enter a hermeneutically sealed environment. It's all hard tomatoes from Spain, apples from South Africa are cheaper than British, milk so cheap it's nearly free, and behold, best of all it won't go out of date for two weeks at least, best buy the bulky carton, look how happy cartoon cows look emblazoned in fields. Everything is so clean, there's no soil, no dirt, the meat is more red than blood, it too verges on the cartoon, bright bright pink the way it looked when I showered after the birth of my first son. Kidneys remind me of haemorrhages best forgotten, it's the closest this flesh gets to authenticity, how we need new words, or new definitions, or both, so we can begin to understand, to be able to read the environment, the signs, the signals, not just the words, not just the easy narrative. How we need to question. Brands proliferate and beg I buy them, it is impossible nearly to avoid Unilever or Nestle or Pepsi Cola. Down the Great Dragon was hurled, this cornucopia of delights, this over production of food that's eating up the earth, the balance of power is tipped when resources used outweigh calorific value, we need new ways to price goods. It's a market economy, what price dairy, sugar and fat? What price comfort? What price modernity? And who pays, when?

This economy does not work, we do well to question exactly what it is we are developing.

There's a strange hum in the shop. As if it's all refrigerated, air pumped in, cooled to a standard temperature, whose standard, whose temperature. If I stay here long enough will I too live forever, will the preservatives leach into me, will they stamp me with a best before, use before? I need a sandwich, New York Deli style pastrami, I do not recall my New York sandwiches being styled as this, but I buy it. I am not sure what's in it, although it lists the ingredients in some sort of code, tells me the fat, the calories, the protein, breaks it down nicely so I can add it to my daily total, and best of all, is in a meal deal, I do not need to part with much to get coke, crisps thrown in. I never have to touch food again to live I realise; I never have to peel, to chop, to work, to understand. It's all right here, every flavour I ever wanted, fusion food fusing until confusingly enough I no longer understand its point of origin, but it's ok, let's appropriate everything we want, let's trample on what we want, because we're worth it. We're all fucking worth it, until we know the price of everything, but the cost of nothing.

It's the hum that gets me, and the child, whinging, begging its mother to get it more hopped up on more sugar, asking for more chemicals needing counterbalanced with more medication, I want I want I want it choruses, more more more. It's this that's making me think this way, I think.

I am light headed; I have not eaten this confused sandwich. The parent snaps a picture of a begging brat, for daddy, for Facebook, and for any, every, stranger who cares to look. I make an escape, blinking in the sunlight. This city does not work.

I could assume this position of cynic, I could excoriate, I could play the misanthrope, and play it well. But this is my city, and I am trapped here in it in this awkward trinity of home, belonging and place. Although I proclaimed otherwise I am of it, I leave it and I miss it, I call it home and mean it. I need it to work; I need these webs not to snap. I need most of all to see it through a more hopeful lens because I cannot comfortably live in it and watch it fail, I need to believe change is possible; I need the clichéd comfort of hope.

To work is a verb, and so denotative of action. But, I'd rather confuse it for a different category of word, I'd rather let it remain passive, for I am, at heart, a watcher. I'd rather watch and lambast and nip to the chip shop than do. But all this watching, observing and recording will do nothing, and so I must become the writer as activist, which means allowing the city to function on different terms. And on practical verbal terms, it means actively doing something to change this stasis of knowing, yet not doing. It means letting myself view the city in a different way - if the city can grow and produce food then it starts to buffer itself, to create resilience - and seeing the green spaces. The hopeful spaces that could become something else, that could be dug up, become fertile growing spaces closing the binary between city and country, feeding the city in practical terms. When the city is seen from above green spaces proliferate in all areas, lessening social inequality - there's as much potential in less privileged areas as in the wealthy ones.

It's daring to imagine a city that works, that can feed itself and its visitors, that trades not only on an imagined past, but on a vibrant present. That dares to hope to breed a new generation of children who understand the actual worth of their food.

It means arming my sons with spades. It means learning how to live.

Note: The book referred to is Michel Faber's *The Book of Strange New Things*

SONNETS TO ROBERT FERGUSSON

◆◆◆◆◆◆◆

DAVID WHEATLEY

i.
Fegs, Rab, fa's thon gowk stravaigin
doon the road, his clart locks shakin
and wheemerin o' his spaul-banes achin'?
    Puir bummer,
dreein a darg o' pratie-howkin
    aa bluidy summer.
Keekin oot frae Auld Meldrum
ye maun hae seen Bennachie's lum
faur a haill clamjamfrie cam
    fer a stramash
in Roman times, lea'in sum
    puir fowk gey hasht.
But fit's that noo stramash I'm hearin'?
Jouk in here, or we're forfaren!

ii.
Some het aquavit'll wet yer thrapple,
I dare say. The weither's aafa dreich:
it's chuckin – *dingin* it doon. My Doric
comes and goes: I'm also nae sae supple
wi' the habbie, Rab; hence these sonnets.
Bank that fire up. Pass me a *Sunday Post*
('Vote No to Save the Union'): let it toast,
its hopes sent up in flames, just like the Nats'.
But what is our nation?, well you might ask now
'14's been added to the bingo card
of Scotland's jackpot years the wrong side claimed,
and Bingo caller Cameron tells us how
the loser gets one Devo Max and, coward
dafties that we are, we throw the game.

iii.
Purple and yellow polka-dot town houses
hewn from every kind of rock do not
this city make, that takes its granite neat
and cuts dead all your garish non-grey choices.
That flash of red's a trawler from Stavanger,
or is it a Tennents T glimpsed through the haar?
There's nary a lantern I'll not follow here,
shipmate, if it means us dropping anchor.
Ah Scotland, deck for the bard fit music hall,
ringing with Burns's lays or pibroch's skreed;
but you've not heard of Burns (though he loved you),
the sailors pile into a strip bar while –
remembering your line that 'music's dead' –
a busking piper hangs his head, soaked through.

iv.
Burns, Rab Burns, makar o' 'Tam o' Shanter' –
thon carle whase statue stands aff Union Street
and whase scunnert, bronze een weel micht greet
like oors for Scotland and the spell she's under.
Westminster warlocks gatherin i' the mirk
gae primpit like the beldams frae Macbeth
and, ech, bite haurd for auld wives wantin teeth –
each uggsome form thrawin off its cutty sark.
The dowie ghaists reek worse than alley cat-spray:
Gordon Broon spoons up his Tory porridge,
Jim Murphy does a turn as Harry Lauder,
Alistair Darling's eyebrows dance the strathspey,
and, what's this, Tony Blair, Bob Geldof, George
Galloway, marching wi' the Orange Order!

v.
But aa Scots sloch aits, scrieved Samy Johnson.
He'll be a lang time ficklin o'er his brose
afore yer haemil leid stairts mouin prose
the like o' whilk the doctor hings his rants on.
Grub Street's 'lexipharian' non-pareil!
Ye didna wiss the Doc tae lear the Scots
mair fantoush, gawsy weys tae dink their thochts,
wi' aye sae mony gleg tongues on the payroll.
There's bings o' Pictish stanes in Auld Brythonic
and Arthur Johnston's Inverurie Latin;
MacDiarmid made his Shetland stanes speak Norn
and Gaelic corrieneuchs are aye a tonic.
But queen o' aa's a tongue mair aften shat on:
this throughother speech, this Scots, in which we're twan.

vi.
Gies your gab, I might say, though another
Robert (Garioch) pulled this trick first, years back.
I bounce my voice off his and get yours back
as well: the banter of aa loons thegither.
I've couthied up across the decades aince
before, Rab, to a countryman of mine,
James Clarence Mangan – have you met? You maun
exchange verse letters or a sonnet sequence.
But ay loons, loons! The only quine you'll find
in Mangan's Róisín Dubh, and Aberdeen's
a statue-park for chain-mailed beardy blokes.
Where's Mother Scotia, 'that beauty lang had kend'?
Sharp on the breeze, a rowst of high-pitched quines
fades to a silent dark beyond the docks.

vii.

Ane place ye'll hear a lassie's voice is sangschaws
doon The Blue Lamp: 'There lived twa sisters
in ane bower...'. Songs whaur hairt-wae festers
wi' unfinished business, sair and anxious.
And someone's for the chop: 'He's coorted the eldest
wi' his penknife...' But then she kills the younger
quine for spite, wha'd ne'er done ocht to wrong her.
Songs that chowk the dulie lungs like coal-dust.
You'd a braw voice for your 'Lassie My Dearie',
but a maiden in song is soon unmade:
the hairt's mair slauchterhoose than nunnery.
Strike up while you can wi' 'Lassie Lie Near Me',
but ballads want blood: 'There's either a maid
or a milk-white swan drooned in the dams of Minorie.'

viii.

Tumblin doon the howff stairs wi' a curt aith
while airtin for the gents', ye end up arselins
i' the strone and gleeked by some coarse loons.
Auld breeks, auld freend throu daftest days o'poortith,
and duddy trooser-seat: fit times ye hae
brookin yer puir *embarras de richesse*
o' aa the jyle cells, bar stuils, braes an ditches
ye've made yer awn throu years o' sons and wae.
Yet part we maun, ye tell yer breeks, then lab
them oot the winda on some housemaid's heid.
Who wears the troosers noo? On my heid too,
amang Edina's roses, yer breeks drop,
and braithing deep the fairty guff ye dreed
I ken the midden whaur aa poems grow.

ix.
Your words to me are 'Caller Water', a *fons*
Bandusiae whose living streams I sup.
Scotland is Greece and Rome: I lap it up,
and dream of lochans thronged with nymphs and fauns.
But these days 'Caller Water' comes in bottles
with Alka Seltzer bubbles for effect,
and nature privatized is nature fucked –
a dying grouse some bastard gillie throttles.
Where wee whaups picked their way on sandy feet
Donald Trump lines up a hole-in-one
and buzzing 'choppers fill the air, not lav'rocks.
Lose 'Caller Water', choose black gold: reboot
as Scotland's corporate Anacreon,
laureate of share quotes, Mercs and oil rigs.

x.
This traipsin's takin affa lang to get
you saufly hame frae Aberdeen to Embra.
Becalmed in this vagabond penumbra
in your brouky claes and buits ye tug at –
a Donside Rimbaud – fit ye need's a hobby.
Have you tried creative writing? 'Unlock
Your Inner Poet', 'Self-Publish Your First Book' –
ye ken the drill – 'Connecting With the Habbie.'
I'd sign you up, but some young poet you are:
nae website, nae on twitter, New Gen reject –
ye're gangin naewey fest. It matters, son;
your retro *maudit* act's fair fooshtit-dour.
I'll do PR, you get your poems rejigged.
We relaunch with: 'The New Don Paterson'.

xi.
Fornenst Dunnottar Castle, history's
a teemit skull, spugs an foumaws threidin
its een like weyrs to stap the sicht they're dreidin
o' yet mair Covenanters, Whigs and Tories.
Lang syne, here sic an sic dang sae an sae:
here hunders birned and stairved and drouned in keech
as God ordained and ministers would preach;
nou as then, the ootleuk's gey wanchancy.
Gin the stanes could speak they'd airt yer glower
to whaur Bill Wallace stuid and bid ye ken
the foumaw's nest they mynd aince on thon swaird,
fer history's the glamour and the glaur
o' ages caldrife tae the works o' men –
a butterfly perked on the Bruce's swuird.

xii.
A butterfly flees aboon Union Street,
where wage slaves, in your day gart to scriven,
dunt at keyboards, data-input-driven.
I follow your words, but all I do's repeat,
repeat, repeat, just like your scratchy quill.
Deposition, divorce and testament –
like art without the rhyme-words at the end –
pile up, words no one reads and no one will.
You write your testament and date it blank.
It's only a convention, after all,
a canty farewell practised like a lesson.
Death, like scrivening, comes down to ink:
a paper signed, you handing me your will
across the desk to copy and pass on.

xiii.

'In the cells': your final tumble ends
not on a stairwell but a Bedlam ward,
whaur manin bare-scud doiterels gae afeart
o' rattons like a plague their last duim sends.
Ane puir quaichin bedlar's Jesus Christ,
anither's Charlie Stewart hissel retoured:
twa keengs o'keengs doverin i' the clart
an keepin up their dirdum till aa's wheesht.
Throu yer snell deid-thraw and fit comes efter
I hear nae cruinin frae the ghaistly choir,
but aye the river o' Scots song flowen away
and spierin doucely as it gaes if there
isna time fer – gie it laldy – ane mair
chorus o' 'The Birks of Invermay'.

xiv.

Yet part we maun, wi' teemit wame,
nae gweed braid claith tae aither's name
an nae mair crack as ye tramp hame,
    forwandert chiel
wi' naewey 'neath the mune's bricht leam
    tae gie ye biel.
Ettlin tae souch fareweel I'm drooned
oot by the traffeck soothwart-boond,
an Aberdein is dreich, dreich grund
    fer a gaun-aboot
wha tholes tho he can scantlins staund
    ilk bygaein plowt,
an hailsed by nae lum's cadgy reek
alane throu wund and mirk maun treik.

SHOP GIRLS OF EDINBURGH

LUCY ELLMANN

Every August, in brand-new boots, the Burry Man stalks the land. He can hardly move, can hardly speak, can hardly see, and certainly can't pee: it would require the removal of his whole costume. So the admirably continent Burry Man walks around South Queensferry offering his blessings and hopes of fertility at every door. He is chased by children, dogs, reporters, and residents who – whether mischievously, considerately, or superstitiously – offer him a dram, which he has to drink through a straw. On and on he wends his lonely way. He has companions to help keep him upright and carry his ornamental branches of foliage, but the Burry Man himself is a solitary figure, a man apart, unreachable, self-contained – like a ripe cheese in its rind – encased and muffled by his barrier of burrs.

The Burry Man is the ovum to the semen of shop girls that springs uncontrollably from every doorway of Edinburgh: the one unique, heroic, intent upon his altruistic task; the other, insouciant, crowdminded, all trying to look alike. These denatured spermatozoa don't exert themselves to meet the egg: shop girls don't want any goddam fertility rites. Babies won't help them. They can't afford babies! So they lounge about dully in sterile sacs (shops), awaiting release of any kind.

◆ ◆ ◆

Here they come, teetering on their six-inch heels, their faces a heavily marketed shade of orange decorated with Cubist mascara work, four pounds worth if a penny, and that's *per eye*. Their legs are splayed, or otherwise displayed, revealing every patellar, fibular, femoral and tibial contour without discrimination, in leggings, tights, or nothing at all – just black-and-white striped crocheted hotpants will do. Apparently. Legs *must* be shown, from top to bottom, it is the Law. The free gawk at so many gams could be of great use to the lovelorn, if they could still love, or art students, if they retained any interest in life drawing, or students of anatomy, were there any left. Or ignoramuses (would that there were fewer).

They work all day long, the shop girls of Edinburgh, sometimes all night too, their lives sacrificed to commerce, from which they themselves benefit not one iota. They spend their earnings on fripperies, booze and tongue studs with which to lure the recalcitrant male – despite the unlikelihood that he will provide the ecstasy they crave. Steinbeck says the men of Cannery Row know more about car mechanics than they do about the clitoris. The young men of Edinburgh are the same, and the shop girls too – they so wearyingly underestimate their own animal potential. But they do understand Kardashian gynaecology, and know Miley Cyrus's butt like the back of their hands. The shop girls of Edinburgh concoct their makeup ideas and other forms of subterfuge as oblique homages to minor celebs, from whom they also learn the marvel of the female stomach made flat.

They zoom around at night, for no reason, inside party buses that ferry them shit-faced from one noisome club to another; they dance, guffaw, glug shorts and pop pills on the top deck in between venues. Here many an unfortunate lifelong allegiance is forged. Later they graduate, from discobus to hen-party limo, in which yet more hilarity is extruded like forcemeat, to the permanent disgust of the drivers and passers-by. Or else they trot along on their trotters, in herds, weaving between rival herds when they meet at the corners. To charge around Edinburgh clutching a five foot-long plastic penis and balls – can this be counted a human achievement? Might make a good Vettriano; not an Ingres.

Where *is* their anger, the shop girls of Edinburgh?

They function without it, the way sightless sideways bottom feeders slide around under the sea to mate, eat and die without light. But the shop girls of Edinburgh are surface dwellers, buffeted between the rocks of repression and oppression – without which these lovely limpets would be lost. The shop girls of Edinburgh find stability in stagnation, and for this win favour in their nation. They shine, in little pools of pointlessness. When they aren't drowning, around midnight, in pools of chunder on the High Street.

The shop girls of Edinburgh live with their parents (who already seem to them decrepit and needy), or with boyfriends, or with other girls. No matter where though, too much of their salaries goes on rent, leaving them, the backbone of finance, to worry non-stop about money. Because the foreign holidays are a must, and the designer clobber, and expensive moisturisers applied to skin already moist. To validate the moisturisers, they smoke, which wrinkles and further impoverishes them.

They sell flowers, marshmallows, cameras, towels, trowels, trinkets, school uniforms – any article of female enslavement. But what is the idea behind putting one lone young woman in charge of an off-licence? Not only do these alco-shop girls have to heft great big boxes of bevvie, they also have to handle rowdy customers, from whom they are expected to protect the *wine:* a new gladiatorial sport. But all the shop girls of Edinburgh are on the front line. Capitalism will keep them squirming all their lives and doing what they're told, as handy little units of wealth-generation and expenditure. For as long as possible, they must remain oblivious to their own power. With the right training in inanity (amply provided by school and home) they are unlikely to overcome their obtuseness. And then there are the added distractions ably provided by the belligerent boyfriends, who want to hit them, scold them, slander them, photograph them in revealing poses, and set fire to their tenement buildings at the least sign of betrayal.

It is their job, the shop girls of Edinburgh, to try not to look dumpy as they trundle through their dumpy town or man the barricades, their shop counters. They are paid for this and while they can't afford their rent, they exert themselves to make a show of splendor (with the help of peer reviews, Facebook advice, and regular hauls from Primark and TK Maxx). So that when the much-prized tourists turn up at the shop, the shop girls seem like shop girls from somewhere slightly more cosmopolitan. Perhaps. Not Edinburgh certainly, this long-forgotten outpost of freedoms nobody wants anymore and literature nobody reads anymore and traditions nobody remembers anymore except for 'Gardyloo!', and oatcakes, in all their hierarchical glory – the fine, the rough, the ready – and the courtly ceilidh kilts that gradually slip down the bums of malted wedding guests.

Yes, these girls are our global representatives, they are made to be pushed around *on a global scale,* made for disaster and terrorist attack. They are made to be run over by the trams their own council taxes paid for. And they must be exported, since it is now essential to fling every living being into orbit around the planet. To travel proves you belong to the human race (the race to use up all the oil as fast as possible and destroy everything).

So the shop girls of Edinburgh, who can't afford their rent, rush to the airport (by tram or bus) and head for some hideous oasis of cliché, where they can get a real sunburn, bother a dolphin, or enrage a Greek. They encounter their shop-girl counterparts across the counters of Abu Dhabi, Dubai, Corfu and Tenerife, before scuttling back to their stations at Jenners, Superdrug and H&M, where they can forget whatever they just discovered in foreign climes, their amnesia reinforced by the miasma of chemical sprays, neon lights and Kleenex. They return to hobbling around at night on broken heels beneath old buildings lit up like fairground rides – this one red, that one purple. Or running away from the (orange) Scott Monument, while lovers and lunatics jump off the top, or yell at them from the Big Wheel. For at night the shop girls of Edinburgh attract men like midgies, annoying and suffocating midgies who cling and buzz and bite the girls and make their lives a misery.

When they retreat from male to female company, the rules are strict. You sit in threesomes outside cafes, pretending not to feel cold as you consume your eggs benedict and iced coffee, blinded by midwinter sun. Three identical plates of eggs benedict in a row, three identical coffees, three identical shop girls spaced evenly on a bench. You sit there exhibiting your blindness to all the people who have to swerve into the street to avoid crashing into your six bare legs and six eggs benedict. After the pedestrians the pavement-tickling machine advances to cast fag filters, sputum and dog shit at your pretty tippy toes, as five thousand cars lurch by. A morning out after a rough all-nighter of pre-loading followed by freeloading: the fake fun of girlie outdoor eating.

From these three wan, worn women in a row emanates of course the rampant joy of being young and female and alive! Or it might, but for the fact they were born into a world that regards all life as valueless. *Except* when humanity can be induced to shove around the pounds and the pence, which is what these girls most characteristically do. They are models of monetary machination.

◆◆◆

Meanwhile on the Water of Leith, unseen, the dipper dips and goosanders gallivant.

◆◆◆

Unresistant, gullible, amenable and unquestioning, the shop girls of Edinburgh are like super-strength paper towels. They absorb everything: Strontium 90, nanoparticles, CO_2; trans fats; bullshit; Jeremy Clarkson, Madonna; vodka, peanuts; the humdrum, the doldrums, drums of any kind; likewise earth tremors, radio waves, microwaves, sonic booms and cosmic rays; romcoms and sitcoms; low-fat milk, additives, MSG, food colourings, trace elements; the fates of rabbits, laboratory beagles, and koala bears; punches, penises, proposals; crime, caffeine, condescension; grime, Clearasil, Neutrogena; all adverts and propaganda; bills of rights, bills of sale; cat dander; the rules of board games; overdrafts; irony. And they have an importance – they and their like across the land decide if a lousy TV show soars or folds.

Depressed though they are, the shop girls of Edinburgh are the optimists without which a species fails. They have nothing whatsoever to be optimistic about. But it is the Law. In a contest between yelling and selling, selling wins: the shops in which they work are calm compared to where they come from. So, to the shops they run, to escape the hoots and brutes. They make their way to and from home deafened by wolf whistles, snipery, sexual bribes and bargains, and the electronic tones of a disembodied female voice naming the bus-stops (just another shop girl made good).

What is their fashionable get-up but an *expression* of noise, of ear-splitting brain clutter? And the wish to be somewhere else, perhaps LA. The more they take in, the less they can think straight (or so our capitalist masters hope). At 4:00 a.m. their drunken boyfriends drive them to Fort Kinnaird for KFC, thereby ensuring that chickens will be tortured for another day. In the KFC factories where their boyfriends may well work, it is *de rigueur* to kick those that are about to die. The customers never notice their fried chicken legs and wings are full of broken bones. It's 4:00 a.m. goddammit, and something instructive could happen to Kim Kardashian at any moment. In lives so starved, so terrible, you cannot afford to miss out on a little *schadenfreude*.

The shop girls of Edinburgh are the battered battery hens of our mercantile enterprises. There they stand all day in cramped quarters, prone to disease, and ruining their ankles. They're cruel and nasty to other chickens. They have been taught from birth to hate themselves, and boy are they good at it., they can hate *anybody* now. And what is there to love? They have a devotion to status, and will ostracise their sisters for wearing the wrong kind of leggings, or turning out to be gay, or unversed in something that's trending. They'd peck them to death for less if they could get away with it – but prison would interfere with work, and work is all they're good for, it's what they live for, breathe for, drink water for. To serve. It's what they dress and eat for, shit and pee for, at pre-arranged intervals during their shifts: there is careful planning involved in the unlikely survival of millions of chickens in their rows.

Squawking, squabbling, scrabbling, gamely they search the merch all day, and are told – by magazines, or phone apps – what to eat for lunch. This is why at 12:50 or 1:10 their talons scrape disconsolately at three grapes, a matchbox's worth of cheddar cheese, two butt-naked rice cakes. Some chockies for dessert can't hurt! Surely. They make up for it with a can of Diet Coke to keep them awake for the next three hours, if indeed they ever sleep, the shop girls of Edinburgh. But who *cares* if they sleep, so long as they keep laying those golden eggs for Debenhams, Currys, and Dorothy Perkins?

They have to be polite, or they'll get the old heave-ho. So all day long the shop girls of Edinburgh pretend to give a damn. In return, they are allowed to live, their clipped and broken wings flapping against each other, their clucks unheard. Deep down, never were people more morose. At night the poor chicks perch on bar stools, all in a row, now caged by circular chit-chat, pat pick-up lines, quotidian drugs and voddie. They sort themselves instinctively into manageable bunches, the better to ease the fears of men who like women in multiples but not multitudes. The hens are there for coupling purposes, after all, and they haven't got all day.

At work they observe the public in all its finery and foolishness. They find it hard to keep a straight face. Drunks come in from the street to cop a feel, or get warm. They ask the shop girls silly questions to spin out the time. But the shop girls save their true contempt for any woman over forty-five, makeup awry or nonexistent, bulges emerging in every direction. The shop girls of Edinburgh cannot imagine such a state of unselfconsciousness. And then there are the more ornate ewes dressed up as lambs, remaindered females emulating whatever leggings-and-tartan-scarf look or drug-mule bun is currently in favour, enhanced by the older woman's superior access to bling. All of it a feeble encroachment on shop-girl terrain.

Yet their own mothers are no different from these sad sack customers, which becomes all too evident when mother and daughter walk down the street together. Before smudgy mirrors in crappy loos, the two masked women paint out the shadows beneath their eyes with fancy concealer products and plough on.

◆◆◆

The secret dreams of shop girls are surely not cars and homes and thugs and kids and Disneyland. No, *this* is the stuff of shop girl dreams:

> to turn somersaults, naked, out of doors, with their cunts in the air
> to wallow in baths of whipped cream and maraschino cherries
> to ride a galloping stallion bareback along the beach at Yellowcraig
> to be immortalized by a stookie, or at least a stooshie, in St Andrew Square
> to understand the phases of the moon and the Dog Star
> to be free as a mermaid adrift in the sea
> to run into a bullring and befriend the bull
> to discover something very, very important, perhaps archaeological
> to speak the language of goats, hoop-snakes, the Burry Man
> to burrow with badgers, dine with dippers, but leave dolphins to their own devices
> to be unique
> to fly
> to hide a pet mouse in their mouths and scare people.

Illustrations by Diana Hope

THE ABOLITION OF THE UNIVERSITY

LOU DEAR

The university has a chequered past. Now, what of its future? Western history paints it in confident brush strokes, from medieval Bologna and the *studia generalia* of the twelfth century to the multi-billion dollar knowledge-producing industries of Harvard and Oxford. But Wendy Brown argues that "broadly accessible and affordable higher education is one of the great causalities of neoliberalism's ascendance in the Euro-Atlantic world." And furthermore, the evolution of neoliberalism from a set of economic policies to a mode of reason and government is radically remaking state institutions and societies in a way that imperils not just liberal institutions, but democracy itself.

In the past year, academics, non-academic staff and students across the UK, Canada, the Netherlands, Ireland, Albania, Finland and elsewhere have staged protests against neoliberal reason and its encroachment on universities. The triggers for these demonstrations and occupations are many: cuts in public funding, privatisation, casualised working contracts, redundancies, restructuring, the purging of subject areas and 'unprofitable' access programmes. The lack of accessibility, the Eurocentric or 'white' curriculum, insufficient representation for marginalised students, rising tuition fees, university investments in fossil fuels, militarized science and technology. Senior management conduct and pay, corporate culture, and the erosion of democracy within the institution, including the disempowerment of academic senates. Education in this environment is not to be considered as a value in and of itself, but simply as a means to accrue human capital.

A more expansive notion of education is threatened by the neoliberal corporate university model. The liberal arts face many threats: forced extinction by government – because they do not serve the market and because they are capable of resisting it – and irrelevance, due to elitism (reduced, as in the Renaissance, to an enclave for the ruling class to govern with more style). When recalling the university as one of the few arenas in modern society in which prevailing ideologies can be rigorously scrutinised, Terry Eagleton asks, "What if the value of the humanities lies not in the way they conform to such dominant notions, but in the fact that they don't?" Indeed, Gayatri Spivak argues that the humanities are the ethical health care of society. But can they live up to this claim?

The history of the university serves as one more brick in the construction of the Master's house: an appropriation of modernity. We must question the university's instituting myths. Walter Rüegg opened his four-volume comparative history of European universities unambiguously: "The university is a European institution; indeed, it is the European institution par excellence." The university is "a community of teachers and taught, accorded certain rights, such as administrative autonomy and the determination and realization of curricula (courses of study) and of the objectives of research as well as the award of publicly recognized degrees, it is a creation of medieval Europe, which was the Europe of papal Christianity."

But there is evidence of advanced centres of learning outside the Middle Ages of Europe in China, India, Sri Lanka, Mesopotamia, Egypt, Greece, Rome, Constantinople, Baghdad, Gaza and other places. Students in Mesopotamia and early Egypt attended classes in advanced studies around 3000 BC. There was a centre for rationalist learning in Baghdad created by the caliph Al-Mamum in the ninth-century, based on the earlier Persian Academy of Gundeshapur. Among many scholars at this 'university' was Mohamad Al-Khwarizmi, the father of algebra and the algorithm. Schools in China conducted exams prior to the formation of the Roman Empire. India's Nalanda preceded Plato's Academy by a hundred years. Nalanda 'university' was said to have thousands of students and hundreds of teachers, and a nine-story library containing hundreds of thousands of books. In the eleventh century the 'House of Knowledge' in Cairo attracted brilliant minds of the age, including Ibn Al-Haytham, who developed theories of optics that laid the foundation for our understanding of human vision.

Convention has it that the universities at Paris and Bologna were the only original universities. The Parisian model influenced Oxford and Cambridge, the rest of Britain and later North America. The Bolognese model shaped universities in Spain, and later, Latin America. But in *The Theft of History,* Jack

Goody contests the notion that higher education started with the founding of the university at Bologna. He alerts us to the takeover of history by the west, in which "the past is conceptualized and presented according to what happened on the provincial scale of Europe, often western Europe, and then imposed upon the rest of the world. That continent makes many claims to having invented a range of value-laden institutions such as 'democracy', mercantile 'capitalism', freedom, individualism. However, these institutions are found over a much more widespread range of human societies."

Since universities have long been associated with the nurturing and advancement of human society and culture, there are obvious reasons why Europe would seek to covet them. But this western-centric discourse is hard to defend. When western Europe fell into obscurity during the Dark Ages, Islamic and Byzantine civilisations and intellectual traditions persisted. By the twelfth century, Islamic intellectual currents which extended from south Asia to Spain had contributed to an awakening in Europe. The Italian Renaissance, which sparked Europe's transition from the mediaeval to the Early Modern period, was assisted by Islamic philosophers and scientists like Ibn Rushd and Ibn Sina.

Goody argues that the Academy and the Lyceum of ancient Greece and the Roman schools in Alexandria, Antioch, Athens, Beirut, Constantinople and Gaza were "effectively the universities of the ancient world". Al Qarawiyin in Fes, Morocco, founded in 859, is the world's oldest academic degree-awarding university; Al Azhar in Cairo, established in 970, the second oldest. Contesting the idea, specifically, that Christian Europe had a decisive role in further higher education institutions, Goody points out that these schools, which were almost all in Asia or Africa, were shut down by Justinian in 529. Christian leaders closed many institutions of higher education before the *studia generalia* of the twelfth century (which provided education for priests and monks) came to the fore. There are examples from Byzantium, Islamic Spain, China and Persia of institutions of higher education which resemble modern universities. Why does the history of the university not refer to them?

Bologna is proffered as the first university because of its age and its unique corporate character. But the suggestion that Bologna was founded in 1088 is attributed to myth rather than historical accuracy (as Roland Barthes suggested, myth works by making the historical seem 'natural'). In his examination of institutions of learning in Islamic societies and in the 'west', George Makdisi says that despite "significant parallels between the system of education in Islam and that of the Christian West", the university was a form of social organisation – the corporation – which was only found in the Christian west. The 'corporation' needs further examination.

The private corporation has a basis in Roman law as a form of political personality with rights and duties of its own. It was never designed to be outside power and authority, but with a degree of separation and detachment. After the collapse of the Roman Empire in the fifth century, the corporation was adopted under the authority of the papacy.

The period in which the university was supposedly set up in Bologna was a time of intense social conflict between the emperor and the Pope. The university was at the apex of this because it taught both canon and civil law. There was a strong pressure on teachers and students to form some kind of organization for protection and mutual support. It was the formation of this safeguard around the community which scholars argue is unique and specific to Europe. This institution was a legal entity, it could hold property and endowments, but what seems most relevant about its specificity is its relationship to power and authority, or its ostensible departure from it. It is claimed that Asiatic, Arabic and Byzantine institutions depended on a prince or emperor, and were thus practically and intellectually constrained.

The corporation has a specific social function, and that social function is inherently conflicted. The values and norms which bind the members of the institution are, necessarily, not homogeneous. The corporate community plays host to 'agonisms': productive adversarial conflict between the academic freedom of the university as a corporate community, the freedom of the individual, collegial solidarity, and the need for autonomy and control from those who supply financial resources. From the beginning of university education a tension developed between the impulse to seek truth and the desire of many to achieve practical skills, a concern very much present today. According to establishment historians of the university, social conflict was fundamental, but structures and mechanisms developed to keep the institution in an open equilibrium, to maintain a space, slightly detached, but ultimately mandated by power.

To some extent the idealised history of the university as a place and space outside power is similar to Eurocentric liberal claims over the public sphere, which began evolving during the Renaissance. In *A Secular Age,* Charles Taylor contends that public space – rather like the university in these historical descriptions – exists "outside power", as "discourse of reason on and to power, rather than by power." However, ever since Jurgen Habermas recognised and theorised the importance of the public sphere, critics have pointed out that it operates through systematic exclusion and thus invariably involves speech by power. This bourgeois notion of the public sphere is an unrealised ideal of Eurocentric liberal democracy. Closer inspection of the evolution of the university-corporation in medieval Europe may suggest that it, too, did not exist outside power. The extent of its relationship to power is critical because it constitutes one of the only significant differences between the European university-corporation and every other higher education institution across the world.

J.K. Hyde described the intellectual scene in Bologna as anarchic rather than hierarchical. The resort to the formation of a corporation, universitas, appeared to be in response to perceived or actual interference first, from authority, but second, also, from local political actors, townsfolk and so on. In reality, a corporate charter carried no more authority than that granted to it by a sovereign, pope or crown. But what such universities did have is a degree of autonomy over internal affairs. The experiences of Oxford and Cambridge are interesting in this regard, as both universities fought to free themselves from episcopal oversight. Cambridge forged two papal bulls in order to win further autonomy, a move not entirely uncommon at the time.

The combined effects of the Great Schism, the emerging popular spirit of nationalism and the power of secular governments changed the relationship between universities and authority in society. By the mid-fifteenth-century the Renaissance, commercial enterprise and changing imperial rule had significant influence. The closer universities got to 'secular' authorities, the less autonomous they were and the more closely they were imbricated with power in society. Universities closely associated with sovereigns became schools for the ruling classes.

The universities were neither founded nor run in the initial spirit of the university-corporation in medieval Europe. This was exemplified by the Tudor kings in England, who had a mutually beneficial pact with the emerging middle classes who profited from colonial commerce. As Edwin Duryea notes, "Chartered corporations played a central role in assuring this royal authority, including that over the universities which prepared an educated manpower to fill positions in the royal administration that managed the affairs of the kingdom."

A series of moves to strengthen royal control over the university fostered increasing dependency throughout the sixteenth and seventeenth centuries. In 1636, William Laud, archbishop of Canterbury and chancellor of Oxford, issued a famous statutory code enforcing the scope of royal jurisdiction by placing university government in the hands of the associated college heads, a group the Crown believed it could control by managing their election through mandates. Duryea: "The remaining vestiges of the universities' medieval independence evaporated. Oxford and Cambridge officially owed their privileges, and, indeed, their corporate life to the King's pleasure."

It's clear that western history of the university will remain untroubled by the great libraries of Nalanda, Córdoba and Alexandria, the great institutions of advanced learning in Bardas or Al-Azhar. But I insist on troubling this illusory edifice. One of the most important elements of the corporation was its alleged relationship to, and ability to achieve distance from, authority and power in society. In reality, this autonomy only existed for a short time (if at all) and by the seventeenth century had been largely impinged upon by the secular authorities. When conflict – between the academic freedom of the university as a community, the freedom of the individual, collegial solidarity, and the need for autonomy and control from those who supply financial resources – disappears, such tensions lose their creative power. Taking this to its logical conclusion, those working in and around the neoliberal university today will surely agree that such conflict, and balance, has been all but lost.

What also seems tantalisingly certain is that according to the necessarily specific Eurocentric definition of what a university is, I am almost certainly not writing this in one now. The modern westernised neoliberal university – in pedagogy, procurement, governance, and relationship to authority and power in society – is a long way from the idealised intellectual sanctuary or hothouse of philosophical agonisms. Therefore, if we are not in a university, where are we? And moreover, before we get too caught up in nostalgia, where do we want to be? The evolution of the university since the sixteenth century is the story of institutional power overlapping with imperial power. The modern westernised university is one which celebrates investment and research in the epistemologies and technologies of 'progress', ergo, extermination and death. The Campaign Against the Arms Trade found in 2012 that Russell Group universities received £83 million worth of funding from private arms companies and the Ministry of Defence for research and development in arms. Yet, for the moment, precarious as it seems, the university also teaches, learns and fosters life, through the practicalities of public law, or oceanography, and through the subterranean depths of the creative arts. My intention is to revisit the history of the university in the west in order to understand how to fight, and what to fight for.

* This is an excerpt from a longer article to be submitted as part of a PhD in Comparative and English Literature at the University of Glasgow. Lou is an aspiring writer from Tayport, Fife.

FURTHER READING Nayef R. F. Al-Rodhan, *The Role of the Arab-Islamic World in the Rise of the West*, London, 2012. | Talal Asad, *Formations of the Secular*, Stanford, 2003 | Roland Barthes, 'Myth Today', *Mythologies*, London, 2009. | Thomas Bender, *The University and the City*, Oxford, 1988. | Wendy Brown, *Undoing the Demos*, New York, 2015. | Edwin D. Duryea, *The Academic Corporation*, New York, 2000. | Terry Eagleton, 'The Slow Death of the University', *The Chronicle of Higher Education*, 2015. | Jack Goody, *The Theft of History*, Cambridge, 2006. | Anis Khurshid, 'Growth of Libraries in India', *International Libraries Review*, 1972. | G. Makdisi, *The Rise of Colleges*, Edinburgh, 1981. | Walter D. Mignolo, *The Darker Side of Western Modernity*, Durham, 2011. | Chantal Mouffe, *The Democratic Paradox*, London, 2000. | L.D. Reynolds and N. G. Wilson, *Scribes and scholars*, London, 1974. | Charles Taylor, *A Secular Age*, London, 2007. | Walter Rüegg, *A History of the University in Europe*, Cambridge, 1992.

STREET MUSIC

JIM GILCHRIST

Clarinettist John Burgess lets fly with an old Sydney Bechet number, and the plangent cadences of 'Petit Fleur' twine through the damp air and into an indeterminate grey sky. Around the outdoor stage, the audience, happed in Gortex or the kind of transparent plastic Mac that suggests forensic experts at a crime scene, applauds gamely through the soft rain. 'Ees Mardi Gras,' Burgess declares between numbers, in a cod-Latino accent and through a chilled rictus of a grin.

It is high summer on the stonefields of Auld Reekie and the opening 'Mardi Gras' of the Edinburgh International Jazz and Blues Festival, a Saturday afternoon when the city's venerable Grassmarket is given over to visiting and local bands playing from temporary stages. It is a convivial event but, even in July, clearly dependent on clement weather to fully succeed. Edinburgh's perfidious climate can give short shrift to the rasher aspirations and pretentions of its citizens, not least those of events organisers. The Mardi Gras can be blessed by sunshine, encouraging a carnival-esque ambience and allowing festival-goers to bask at tables fringing the bars and restaurants that have proliferated in what has become, superficially at least, the most Continental-seeming of Edinburgh urban spaces. This afternoon, however, the ardour of Edinburgh *en fête* has been dampened somewhat, the city besieged by North Sea haar.

Haar, as we all know, reduces townscape to stage set, eliminating perspective and truncating towers and spires. This particular example isn't as thick as some; it hasn't quite reduced visibility to such a degree that 'scarce might any man espy ane other the length of twa butts,' as John Knox gleefully reported the weather conditions surrounding the arrival at Leith, in August 1561, of his arch-adversary, Mary, Queen of Scots. It is thick and damp enough, however, to lick a gloss on the cobbles, while the looming bulk of the Castle, the omnipresence

---

1 Grassmarket musicians during the 1930s, from left: and 1: Harry Nolan, violin; Sammy Pacitti, guitar; Louie Peruzzi, banjo; Laverno Fenelly, clarinet.

against which the Grassmarket nestles, graduates into nothingness like an ill-defined legend. Bemused tourists gaze up in wonder as the volcanic plug on which the castle perches fades upwards into the grey-out, while Burgess's determined torrent of sinuously reedy melodies, so redolent of more colourful and presumably warmer scenarios – 'Riverboat Shuffle', 'New Orleans Stomp', 'Down Among The Sheltering Palms' – is similarly subsumed into the damp air.

In curtailing the visible townscape, the sea fog heightens the immediacy of whatever remains visible, and perhaps also stimulates memory and something more, so the divisions between layers of time and history blur, just as ephemeral figures fade in and out of vision. This particular Edinburgh enclave is rich in associations for me: my mother, Mary McKernan, grew up here, in a Scots-Irish-Italian community that knew considerable hardship, but also had its own music.

Listening to the defiantly cheerful swing of Burgess's trio and, clashing faintly from behind, the harmonica squall of a blues band drawing its own crowd further down the street, my thoughts turn to a couple of black and white photographs that hang above my desk as I write this. They date from the 1930s and portray a quartet described simply as 'Grassmarket musicians'. Three of them are immigrant Italians – Sammy Pacciti, Louie Peruzzi and Laverno Fenelly. The fourth member is my late uncle, Harry Nolan, second-generation Irish but who married an Italian, Nellie Marandola from Cervaro, with whom he lived in the Grassmarket.

In one of the photographs, Harry is wielding a tenor saxophone, in the other he has a fiddle tucked under one arm. The other three also switch instruments between photographs, between them toting a reed 'n' string ensemble of accordion, banjo, sax, clarinet and guitars – one of which is an intriguing instrument with what look like additional strings extended on a secondary narrow neck. All four musicians sport matching berets and floppy white open-neck collars over dark jackets. They have a distinctly continental café look to them, but what on earth did they play, and what did they sound like? I'm told they cut what would have been a shellac, 78rpm record in a local music shop, but know of no surviving copies. I'd I love to have heard them, this wonderfully exotic, street-baroque-looking quartet emerging from the stacked grey tenements.

In his recently and sadly posthumously published collection of tales, Edinburgh Old Town: *Journeys and Evocations* (Luath Press) the late John Fee, the Grassmarket's celebrated storyteller and historian, describes how the Italian community brought their music – and their instruments – from their hillside towns to Edinburgh's streets: 'Many of these instruments had been handed down through family generations together with the skills required to play them. Mandolins, guitars, fiddles, harps, trumpets and piccolos – instruments that had been played in their village and small town bands, played at births, weddings, funerals and festivals.'

Fee, who knew my mother's family, describe those musicians as playing everything from the operatic arias of Verdi and Puccini to Neapolitan and Sicilian folk songs, and he name-checks some of the families who nurtured this music, some members of whom peer out from those photographs.

I was sent the pictures by one of Harry's sons, Peter, long domiciled in Canada. Harry taught himself the saxophone, and received some violin lessons from local Italians. He played in ballroom dance bands, busked in Princes Street and the music coursed on through his DNA. Another son, Charles, would become a classical violinist, playing in the Royal Philharmonic and Royal Opera House orchestras, while his son, also Charles, would takes his place among the violins of the London Symphony and London Philharmonic orchestras.

My mother, who died in 2005 at the age of 92, told me that during the summer Harry and his Italian bandmates would take the ferries over to the then popular Fife resorts of Burntisland and Kirkcaldy and play to the holiday crowds. But theirs was by no means the only music in the Grassmarket.

Born in 1912, at the foot of Heriot Bridge before the family moved across the 'Market to Thompson's Pend, a tenement and pend long demolished and replaced in the 1970s with a housing association development, my mother grew up amid hard times, although as children, she always said, they didn't know it. In the flat above them lived her beloved Granny Nolan, on whose wall hung a fiddle, and in leisure moments either Harry or her Uncle Jimmy – another fiddler, who also lived in the stair, would strike up a tune and the cry would be 'Face me up!' as she and one of her sisters or friends would dance. In the absence of fiddle-playing uncles, Granny Nolan would simply diddle the requisite tune.

When my mother was about ten the family moved out of Thompson's Pend and up the Vennel to a now demolished section of Heriot Place, overlooking the Flodden Wall that separated them from the more privileged realm of George Heriot's School – a baby sister had died and her mother, she reckoned, simply wanted out of the old house. For surviving children, however, the Grassmarket was a world of Italian organ grinders and hokey-pokey men who stabled their ponies at the Cowgate end of the 'Market while the Corporation had their own stables in King's Stables Road. The horse fairs which used to cram the place with massed, gleaming flanks – as famously painted by James Howe early in the 19th century – had finished just before my mother was born, but she still remembered heavy hoofs sparking off the cobbles as the occasional tinker dealer would run a horse up and down the cobbles to clinch a sale.

John Fee writes in another book, The Grassmarket: *A Place to Live* (which remains unpublished though a bound copy is available in the Central Library's Edinburgh Collections): 'Youngsters in the street in the Twenties and Thirties knew which back yards the various horses were stabled in – often behind the tenements they lived in ...' Such was my mother's experience.

The children ranged over the market and played, illicitly, up the sloping back greens of neighbouring 'superior' tenements, and further up in the airy reaches of Johnston Terrace and the Castle Esplanade. The boys played street football, my mother recalled, posting a look-out who shouted 'Shote!' (pace Robert Garioch's 'Fi'baw in the Street'), should a polisman heave into sight. The girls skipped through shrill games of peevers until they tired of it and scattered, leaving their often elaborate 'peever beds' chalked out on the suddenly silent causeys, as inscrutable as Nazca lines.

In my own more recent history, a piping teacher, doing his patient best to inculcate in me the essentials of strathspey playing, told me they should be played snappily – 'like a wee lassie stoatin' a ba' aff a wa". The admonition stuck, compounded by inherited memory, so that whenever I try, with recalcitrant fingers, to coax a strathspey out of a chanter, the image that comes to mind is of my Mother as a wee girl, stoatin' that apocryphal ba' off the weathered old sandstone wall on the east side of Castle Wynd.

Granny Nolan would take her to hear concert parties at Baillie Barrie's Mission at the top of the Grassmarket – you took your own mug for a cup of tea and they gave you a bun, and you were further serenaded by Barrie's silver band which would play on the Mound, but also at the top of the 'Market.

There must have been a brass or silver band, surely, at the stone-laying for the Salvation Army Women's Hostel at the foot of the Vennel, that steep artery connecting the Grassmarket and West Port with the heights of Lauriston. Sidling through the Mardi Gras crowds, vintage jazz still within earshot, I cross the road over to the red sandstone building, now a rather more privileged backpacker's hostel, and inspect one of its four officially laid stones dating from February 1911, inscribed with the names of Mrs Bramwell Booth, wife of the Salvation Army's founder, Lord Provost William Brown and the reverends A Wallace Williamson and Alexander Whyte, minister of St Giles and principal of New college respectively. None of the stones bears the name of my maternal great-grandfather, Charles Nolan, a journeyman stonemason, reputedly blackballed for union activity in his native Ireland. Having come to Scotland, according to family lore the only identifiable building he was known to have worked on was that Salvation Army hostel.

Until a decade or two ago, of course, it was by no means the only lodging house for the homeless in the area, which could boast a litany of them – the Grassmarket Hostel, the Castle Trades, the 'Vicky' just off in Merchant Street ... Today's 'Market may be the place to go for eating, drinking and upmarket shopping, not to mention the occasional jazz, but, behind the outdoor restaurant tables, the Grassmarket Mission still has its work cut out dealing with the homeless, the hungry, the excluded and the addicted.

Historically, there were other Grassmarket sounds, from 17th century strolling 'mountebanks' to the 'back green singers' my mother recalled who sang for a piece or anything that could be spared during the lean times of the General Strike. If the 'Market was built as a place of hewn stone, something that for centuries cast a grim shadow over these stones was the looming timber of the gibbet where, among many others, more than 100 Covenanters were executed there during the 'killing times' during the latter half of the 17th century. Today, not far from where that blues band is letting rip, a circular memorial plaque evokes the terminal psalms of the martyrs rising into the air.

    Another who later swung there, in 1734, was certainly a musician, Robin Oig MacGregor, wayward son of Rob Roy, accused then of abduction but better known to modern readers, thanks to Robert Louis Stevenson, as the piper, albeit with a price on his head, with whom Alan Breck fights a bagpipe duel in Kidnapped. Breck, initially ready to draw swords with the MacGregor, ultimately concedes to his superior skill: 'Ye have mair music in your sporran than I have in my head!'

    Fiddle music comes to mind yet again, although my memory is imperfect as to whether it was in the White Hart, which has weathered time, mobs and Zeppelin bombings, or in the neighbouring and appropriately titled Last Drop that, one Edinburgh Festival, I walked in to discover the late Johnny Cunningham, demon fiddler and raconteur, hard against the bar, fiddling furiously to make himself heard alongside half of a visiting antipodean pipe band.

    Such echoes never quite fade. One final gig: it's a cold December's night several years ago in The Lot, a former gothic church at the base of the castle rock which became a popular music venue, now sadly defunct, and I'm listening to the superb multinational trio of Tommy Smith, Arild Andersen and Paolo Vinaccia. Just yards from where my Mother grew up in circumstances which would have rendered laughable the very idea of paying to attend a concert, I'm beguiled by Andersen's loop-sampled bass harmonics which shimmer and sigh like the opening of some magic portal. A Scots saxophonist, Norwegian bassist and Italian drummer, gathered here in the Grassmarket, their music is highly cosmopolitan contemporary jazz, with folk strains, and it naturally puts me in mind of that 'Grassmarket band' of immigrant Italians and my uncle Harry, son of an immigrant Irish stone mason.

Once again I find myself wondering what that other band sounded like with its gloriously mongrel assembly of reeds and strings. When I emerge from the Lot, the late-night 'Market has been happed in frozen fog, a few revellers lurching in and out of vision like roistering ghosts, the Castle's lights a corner-of-the-eye glimmer far above, as faint as the Pleiades.

In such conditions any demarcation between the real and the imagined can waver: the Grassmarket becomes a state of mind. Is that the steady tap of Major Weir's staff I hear, as the supposed necromancer, sentenced in 1670 to 'be strangled and burnt between Edinburgh and Leith', descends grimly down what remains of the West Bow, or is it just the sound of a wee lassie stoatin' a ba' aff a wa'?

2 Grassmarket musicians : Harry Nolan, saxophone; Laverno Fenelly, saxophone; Sammy Pacitti, accordion; Louie Peruzzi, guitar.

UNTETHERED

JAMES KELMAN

Then I saw the field.

How many days had I been here? Now I saw it, and knew that I could walk to it. There was no reason why I couldnt except I couldnt. I might walk to there. But I could not.

Had I no power? Had they stolen everything? It wasnt a dream. I was taken and I could not move. I could not move. Is that a joke? It seems like a horrible irony.

I didnt enter that so-called field and I wouldnt enter. Was it mathematical? One day two day, then three, four and coming now to the tenth day, my senses said no, I was not going to be controlled by these damn forces. You know, fuck! It was not to happen. I was not going to allow it to happen.

What to dominate? Or even me; me to dominate. Okay I know myself and know my capabilities. I can rise to the occasion. Of course I can. If they thought I couldnt, if they thought that man they were wrong, they certainly were wrong. I would have challenged them there and then. I always challenged them anyway, I didnt worry about that.

Why could I not enter that field? That to me was like a religious question, certainly logical, as though a logical field, therein the key man that is what I was thinking

You know I didnt have any trust in them. Why ask? No faith, nothing. Of course not. It was only a political position; there is no thing other than that, no morality, no goddam fuck all man so I did challenge them, and challenged them on that. Always. My very existence. There and then at that damn time man right in front of that so-called field, their so-called field, you know, what did they think! Make it a question and I shall answer: Of course, of course I saw it.

Were I allowed. I am not allowed. Even this, to have challenged them on this very point. Prove it! I shouted at them. Prove it to me. As of right you have got no authority. Any power you have you have stolen, you have stolen from people; peoples, plural. All the people of the world. I shouted that to them.

But something was spinning. Near to me. What is spinning? My fucking head! I could not discern. Was it near to me? Spinning near to me, if it is near to me.

I had to search. Then give in to it. If I had to sleep then remain where I was. It was no chair. It was no chair. Damn chair man it was not a chair. I know what a fucking chair looks like.

My finger too, fitting snugly; into my nostril, my ear, between the fifth and third toes of my right foot. That was my finger, talking about my finger, how come? The point of consciousness. I was not being tortured.

Where now here now. Such reflection My feet were bare. I might have laughed at that. Even being there, and that field, what was that field, did I see a field? is this significant? or was it so? I thought Yeh, none of this is by chance.

A time passed. I rose from my chair. It was a chair!

My thoughts no longer raced ahead. What is reflection?

I would not have believed it possible. The place itself, the surroundings, these had changed me. And these long weeds, long long weeds, each time I saw them I wanted to lay me down to sleep, not even to sleep but lying there, with the long stalks, angling above to enclose me. This was a proper field. It had grass rather than symbols, a natural form, if logical.

I knew what to believe. They told me. It was a command. Believe what you know. Such was their advice. These bastards had no shame. They said to me: You have nothing.

I didnt seek information. They gave me it, what they wanted me to know. I preferred to discuss death and that other concept, that concept uhh humiliation; humiliation, of a people, peoples the world over.

I should not have acquiesced. If I did acquiesce. My reaction was if believing what you know was the more important, which surely it was

What followed. I can not remember.

But my reaction then was less than immediate. I acquiesced. I agreed to my own, my own

I do not accept 'degradation'. If the field was there to be entered.

What is a field? A simple area, bounded area. I too was bounded, I too am an area. My body is a fucking map of fucking humanity. Who is to deny that? The degradation that I suffer is the degradation of humanity.

If the affirmative can one deny it? Would one deny it? I put thoughts up to thwart more difficult thoughts you know and mediocrity, mediocrity is not the result.

Although one may predict the unlikely, as to the nature of it, grasping that, it is not feasible. Or is this also a banality, rooted in tautology. We go back and go back, and again.

The mind of a human being, this human being.

The field.

How many days? I think of days man I dont know and I am here and facing the field and I can enter, I could enter and I fucking do not man it is like the one and only the sole thing man, that area of conflict, ultimate one.

The brain is also composed, its constituents, each a field, stalks, weeds

One is commanded not to think but not to think becomes to not think which is activity of a cerebral kind. Thought in itself. My state is secular. And if I am part of a community, of a class or a caste, ethnic or communal division: state of mind. It is a fucking state of mind man I can forget what I am, a fucking human being man part of fucking humanity, of peoples, an individual.

I smile. I smile at these things. These things; such things. 'Such things' is discriminatory. I might have chortled, chortled equalling to laugh aloud in an ironic manner, a manner approaching sarcasm, sarcasm – if not internalized to the extent it had to be. In order to exist it begins from internalization. The challenge is within me. My inner form is logical, not mathematical.

But what meaning does this have? Something lodged, existing within. A thing of myself, purely of myself.

The inquisitors. Those who foment

What is inhumanity? I do not fucking know what it is man I do not know what the fuck it is.

The gaolers cannot control this, you men of the state. Chortling is to be of humanity. Pushing authority, pushing

To be alive is the assumption of control, for this is reflection.

So the place had changed me. This was the fact, how do they say it, these

FOLK WORK FILM

KENNY MUNRO

FOLK, WORK, FILM

> 'For in and out, above, about, below,
> 'Tis nothing but a Magic Shadow-show,
> Play'd in a box whose Candle is the Sun,
> Round which we Phantom Figures come and go.'
> – The Rubáiyát of Omar Khayyám.

Each time I watch a piece of historic archive film I'm startled, transported and encouraged to believe that these folk captured by the camera are still alive. Omar Khayyám expresses the reality. However the figures immediately assert their personality, gesturing to the camera, or conversely are seen as indivisible from the landscape and work in which they're employed. Their spectral presence can be perceived as secondary to the manual process or function of the equipment they're manipulating.

Regional documentary film has recorded folk at work in mining, fishing, farming and in manufacturing. John Grierson and his sister Ruby helped launch the local and international significance of cinéma vérité.

> 'We believe that the cinema's capacity for getting around, for observing and selecting from life itself can be exploited in a new and vital art form'
> – John Grierson

The energy of folk from every walk of life, in that era eighty years ago, is reanimated in celluloid. As voyeurs we enter the time portal of film and identify with the effort and drama of people at work and play. The importance of these 'film-poems' and vignettes of social history cannot be overestimated. They are not a rose-tinted view of arcadia, but employment often verging on servitude, at home and in the workplace; they capture something essentially human & ritualistic which has been lost. The real quality of certain impressions can be difficult to separate from nostalgia. The confident expressions of communal living are often woven into forms of feudalism on the land; being indentured and lashed by the elements of nature, working with few safeguards, dicing with dangerous machinery. But this visceral engagement with work can all be seen as a potent filmic 'story-board' of life.

With these travails it's little wonder that seasonal pageants and festival holidays were enjoyed with such relish and vivid abandon. Civic gatherings also became a forum for promoting businesses using highly elaborate mobile displays, all experienced as a kind of 'theatre' on the day. Films of such pageants could be copied, offering repeat-plays alongside promotion of culture and commerce.

This portrayal of life and determinism embraced by our families forged society's character from rural farm steadings and crofts to an intense habitation in the industrial metropolis. Progressively more people moved to towns seeking a regular pattern of work with steady income, routinely supplemented by migrant workers. The films are punctuated and enriched by the mix of language, customs and symbolism expressed by seasonal celebrations, festivals and gala days, often emphasized within close-knit coal mining communities.

◆◆◆

My early years and family background in the 1950s were centred in Musselburgh & Fisherrow, on the outskirts of Edinburgh, prospering with an economy of fishing, farming and mining.

My family consisted of engineers, stone masons, musicians and traders. We lived minutes from the beach and Fisherrow, the 'back sands', which drew me, as an eight year old, to explore the mysteries of the water's edge of the river Forth. Here nature and technology met around the once viable harbor. For me, play took many forms: trying to spear flat fish, searching for edible crabs or building a driftwood fire, and melting old lead fishing net weights. Were these part of an innate ritual? Laying out empty halves of mussel and cockle shells on the sand, I poured the silvery molten liquid from the tin can into these most ancient of nature's moulds.

Films of the period show a community emerging from economic depression galvanized by the establishment of Musselburgh's Honest Toun Association, launched with the *Riding of the Marches* pageant of 1935, which was captured on film. Films of social gatherings like this were intended to be screened to local audiences in cinemas or community halls. This guaranteed a full house who were excited to see themselves on the 'silver screen' before the feature film. For decades *going to the pictures* was an important recreation in most communities, an experience that created work for some and addictive leisure for others, open to all who could spare a few pennies or a couple of empty jam jars to barter for entrance to the *picture palace*. This is exactly how local boy Bill Douglas started his film education. He went on to create his autobiographical *Trilogy*, shot in the 1970s. Conversely, in the 1930s on the western island of Eriskay, Werner Kissling created a seminal film capturing the poetic lives of the Hebridean community. Film is indeed *a place where extremes meet*.

The filmic experience is part of the remote way we often experience the culture of work in communities, a celluloid back-catalogue of animated life which now has local and international significance.

I recently discovered a tattered printed program in Musselburgh from 1935 which reveals an avalanche of American feature films which were screened three times a week in the 'Honest Toun'. Such titles as *Romance in Manhattan* with Ginger Rogers, *Car 99* with Fred McMurray and Bing Crosby in *Here is my Heart*. Each of the three picture houses advertised a 'full supporting program' in which I imagine newsreel and locally generated documentary films would be presented. We know that this exposure to Hollywood made a huge shift in Scottish life, aspirations and especially tastes in music. America's role in World War Two ingrained that forever.

The British Empire offered major trading opportunities. The Empire Marketing Board was established in 1926. This coupled with a social conscience brought John Grierson to conceive his treatise on the principles of documentary filmmaking.

◆◆◆

Three films portray the 1930s and 1940s as possessing a powerful level of communal spirit and dependency, driven partly by war effort, food production and fund-raising, energizing the kind of community spirit which often struggles to flourish nowadays, but manifests itself as a new appetite for democratic empowerment.

The first film follows the Fisherrow herring fleet; the second explores processes of wire production at the Brunton mill; and then there is the *Riding of the Marches* parade, a grand theatrical procession expressing civic pride, an idyllic scene with throngs of folk cheering it through the streets of Musselburgh. Metro-Goldwyn-Mayer would have been impressed by the quality and scale of the production.

We are able to see these films now due to digital conversion and restoration. Many were silent, but by the mid 1930s professional films had soundtracks and older films were often re-edited with new voice-overs that gave additional context. I prefer the original film edit, even if it is silent. Innovators such as Robert Flaherty with his film Moana (1926) and Sergei Eisenstein's *Battleship Potemkin* (1925), both inspired Grierson. One of his earliest films, with Edgar Anstey, required strapping himself and camera to the wheelhouse of a storm tossed Leith fishing boat, the Isabella Grieg, when he made his early masterpiece entitled *Granton Trawler* in the North Sea.

Grierson and his sister Ruby, plus the intrepid Jenny Gilbertson, inspired those that made films about Musselburgh and across Scotland. Many created by Alec Lowe, connected to an affluent business family who promoted innovative agriculture techniques.

These Lothian films provoke questions about how the role of work in society has evolved and how it has forged our character and been influenced by ritual and the tradition of visual story telling. We are now forced to consider the evidence of what material has survived and its current contribution to our current perception of work – what are the ingredients for a vibrant society?

1. **The Sea:** The Fisherrow Fleet – Musselburgh - Silent
   Filmed by Alec Lowe in the late 1930s

Fisherrow's fishing fleet is commencing its seasonal trip via the Forth, Clyde & Crinan canals to fish for herring in the Clyde estuary and the Minches. Lowe's stunning colour film has a diffuse, painterly quality and depicts folk of all ages in buoyant mood as the fleet prepares for the journey to their base at Rothesay on the Isle of Bute.

You witness a joyful scene at an aquatic social gathering where a man dances for the camera and raises his hat as part of a play-acting performance, with groups of waving observers, setting the mood for a maritime family picnic. Folk crowd the harbour walls, an old steam crane puffs in the background and families sit on the decks of boats which are spic and span as they prepare to depart for part of the journey west. At Grangemouth or Bo'ness the families disembark and return home, allowing the convoy of beautiful boats to navigate the canal locks, heading for the Clyde.

Many films were commissioned for the Glasgow Empire Exhibition in 1936. One, notably entitled Sea Food, shows scientific work undertaken by marine survey vessels, studying fish stocks, migration patterns and plankton distribution. Science and the management of fisheries were being applied, as the concern was that herring stocks were diminishing fast. Compton Mackenzie, John Lorne Campbell and later Frank Fraser Darling expressed their concerns about ecology and sustainable control on fishing in coastal waters.

Interdependent relationships were inevitable. Stewarts & Co. in Musselburgh grew to become one of the biggest national manufacturers of fishing nets.

Boat building was an intrinsic part of the economy. Also barking (preserving) of sails, nets and ropes required importing large quantities acacia cutch/tannin from India. Soaking in the boiling resinous liquid created the distinctive dark red colour associated with preserving canvas sails, sisal ropes and nets – an essential ritual until the advent of polypropylene.

Many of the sculptural wooden fishing boats sported varnished hulls of light wood, with red and black lining along the hull, and wheelhouse with dedicated gilded calligraphy. These works of art were made locally with evocative names such as *Golden Effort, Better Hope and Confidence.*

Around twenty six fishing boats operated out of Fisherrow, before World War Two, for herring, white fish and sprats. Anstruther was still a major port; many towns, St. Monans, Cockenzie and even Kinghorn had been major ship building communities. Harbours were hubs of economic life with ancient traditions. Scenes captured negotiating the canals present domestic chores such as peeling tatties on deck, in counterpoint to working the lock-gates, then playing cards while smoking a pipe. These are relaxing vignettes in what was a challenging profession.

Intriguingly, some of these wooden boats were requisitioned by the Navy in the Second Word War; *Better Hope and Confidence* ended up in Colombo, Ceylon, never to return.

2. **The Machines:** Bruntons Wire Mill – Silent
   Produced by Ronald L Day in the late 1920s/early 1930s

A film from the earlier 1930s promoting the Park Mall works of the Brunton Wire Mill, the major employer in Musselburgh from the 1870s till its closure twenty years ago. Woman and men can be seen working at distinct tasks within, I imagine, a hostile, noisy environment.

This compelling film leads us through the wire-making process, white hot billets of iron manhandled with tongs as they are compressed and extruded through endless smoking machines. The camera is simply the observer, with no visual contact made between worker and viewer. A process-led film in which we are immediately drawn into the remarkable action, a ballet of man & machine. Like a tortured dance, two men systematically guide the spaghetti-like lengths of wire, twisting and turning as they grab the animated looping strips of steel. One imagines squealing sounds of the forged wire, rotating wheels and presses, and the exertion required in pushing ingots into red hot guiding lines, transformed into successive gauges which extrude the wire to the thickness required.

With jump-cut sequences we see large gyroscopic spools of wire rotating at speed, twisting as cables are contorted into a taut coil. Another scenario reveals fine reels of wire being threaded from one machine to another by women with dark work coats and bobbed hair. During World War II the factory ran seven days a week and it is said that some shift workers rarely saw sunlight or the natural world.

Much of the wire rope from Bruntons served the engineering of bridges, maritime vessels, and provided control cables for civilian and military aircraft. The only element of the business which remains in Musselburgh is Brunton Aerospace, the Park Mall works now demolished and replaced by Tesco.

3. **The Pageant:** Riding of the Marches 1935 - Silent

This black and white film is technically one of the best. Well shot from various locations, it records a vast procession of horsemen and women in period costume, the annual Riding of the Marches. A cavalcade of local business and tradespeople, often on horse drawn carts or floats, it shows a spirit of enthusiastic citizenship which most towns with mixed economies

experienced. The spectacle is based on the ancient tradition of redefining territorial boundaries by groups of riders on horseback, the 'Common Riding'. Despite this national tradition, so much public land has been poached!

The parade is led by an armour-clad equestrian figure, the Town Champion, and his attendant, followed by the provost and dignitaries in top hats. Then trades, guilds and business persons of every type symbolize the economic and cultural wealth of the town, represented in elaborately decorated floats and vehicles of

every type. There are pedestrians, cyclists and bands on horseback, followed by weird groups of what look like butchers in top hats, wielding large wooden cleavers and bearing heads of bulls and sheep. They might easily have been carried triumphantly by Roman Legions two millennia before.

Humour and alcohol are no doubt not far away – after the coach with the provost and town councilors pass there is much gesticulating; one can guess the meaning. Then several hundred participants process through the Honest Toun: a pennyfarthing cycle passes; a truck with forge and farrier on back, hard at work; a building company with a large model house; a massive wooden horse topped with what could be Godiva or a Celtic god! It's an almost never ending stream of celebration, marketing, joyous revelry and an intense sense of pride. The mine rescue team, with a section of arched steel tunnel depicted in a truck, make it clear that 'coal was king'.

The 'Fisherman's Walk' is also represented, with men and women symbolically dressed: men with gansies and bunnets and the women in exotic striped dresses, distinctive aprons and colourful scarves, a tableau which would easily be recognised by a Dutch or Baltic community in the 18th century. (I remember in the early 1960s some of these women still carrying basket creels on the buses. The aroma of 'sea-food' was potent!)

I like to believe that my eleven-year-old father is in the crowd with his three brothers and sister – his dad was leader of the town's volunteers brass band. Oh to have been on the street that day in 1935!

ADVENTURES IN AUSTERITANIA

◆◆◆◆◆◆◆◆◆◆◆◆◆◆◆◆◆◆◆◆◆◆◆

EDDIE GIBBONS

COMPUTER OBSTRUCTED DESIGN

The question used to be: *2B or not 2B?*
A pencil, a set square, you were set fair
for the work at hand; drawing on the long apprentice-
ship, the day release scheme and endless night schools.

Then Computer Aided Design threw everyone
into disarray and dunced us in our middle
ages. The wages were going to the younger lads
schooled only in keyboard craft, strangers

to the factory graft we'd cut our teeth on.
Drawing boards disappeared overnight.
A blight of acronyms withered away our work –
IT was training CADDS & DOGGS.

No longer masters of the tools of our trade,
new languages were needed. Computer illiterate,
we were forced in silent droves to draw the dole
and try to square all those vicious fiscal circles.

EARLY MORNING, WEST HARTLEPOOL, 1963
(from the photo with the same title by Don McCullin)

A pipe fitter's mate at the gates of dawn
Is wrenched from sleep by a sulfurous smell.
At six a.m. he'll be entering hell
With the whole damn nation following on.
He's breathed the acids that chimneys discharged,
Winced as the chemicals scoured every cell
Of his threadbare lungs, coughed up, cursed Brunel,
Whitworth and Watt for the shackles they forged.
He's walked this factory road for years, the depth
Of his soles erode with each step, the worth
Of this graft from indenture to death
Shows paltry returns for his time on Earth.
Windpipe-stripping smoke rasps his every breath.
The brass in the south. He's walking north.

ADVENTURES IN AUSTERITANIA

Austeritania (aka 'The Brutish Isles')
is famous for its bakeries and literature;
Jane Austere's *Mother's Pride & Prejudice*
being a prime example of writing from
the quills and inkwells of the upper crust.

Isambard Kingdom Bunuel's *Bridge de Jour*
and *The Discreet Charm of the Broad Gaugee*
are considered masterpieces of Netflix,
though his controversial film *An Andalusian Dogger* has been wheel-clamped
and withdrawn from circulation.

SNP Sturgeonia, formerly Scotland, gave
the world pennycillin, the universal cure
for skin flints, and Trainspotting: the curious
custom of applying adhesive dots to locomotives,
which many view as a protest against the rectilinear
constraints imposed by the traditional tartan tea cosy.
Its National Anthem is, of course, *We Fuel Britannia*.

Austeritania came into being after the *Hundred Day War* in 2015, following the re-election of
the Con & Self-servative party, and the subsequent
referendum to withdraw the Untied Kingdom
from the Eurovision Thong Contest.

Unfettered by any plausible opposition from
south of the border, the Tory hordes wrote
the storyboards for the screenplay of the new
order we now live in: *Austerity Bites,* showing
for more than 1000 nights at a Food Bank near you.

A WORLD IN ACTION

ELIZABETH DARLING

1 A Performance by the Children of the St Saviour's Child Garden in the Gardens of Chessel's Court (courtesy OSP Archive)
2 Children of the St Saviour's Child Garden at Play (courtesy OSP Archive)

A WORLD IN ACTION: WOMEN'S WORK AND CHILDREN'S WORK IN THE CANONGATE'S ST SAVIOUR'S CHILD GARDEN, 1906 – 1914

They are striking images. We notice first the backdrop of Salisbury Crags; next the chimney stacks, oast houses, the walls and roofs of densely-packed buildings. We are in the early twentieth-century Canongate – circa 1910 – a still industrial landscape in which breweries and gasworks jostle for space either side of the steep road that leads up to the Castle and down to Holyrood.

Look again and we see something rather different. Within this grimy urban scene is a garden in which children, the eldest no more than seven, are shown at various pursuits. In the first image, we watch them at some sort of performance, as does the small audience in the shelter nearby. In the second they are at play, concentrating hard on the moves that they execute.

The dissonance between industrial landscape and children at their games is remarkable, but what we see is not the result of an Edwardian version of Photoshop. Rather the photographs document one especially innovative component of the wave of social and urban reform which was aimed at the poor who then worked in the Canongate, and lived in the slums that had been made of its once fine houses.

Such work is usually associated with the metropolitan clearance and improvement programmes of the City Council (much influenced by its Medical Officer of Health, H.D.Littlejohn), or the Conservative Surgery approach developed by Patrick Geddes. But there were others who worked to effect change in the Old Town, among them the young woman in the centre of the photograph of the children at play. By telling her story and that of the kindergarten she founded (for that is what the photographs depict) my aim is to show how often it was in those pre-welfare state days that women initiated acts of social and urban reform and which, in this instance, placed the Canongate at the forefront of the most progressive welfare work of the period.

These ventures were less often manifested in dramatic demolition and new building, and more often took the form of working within existing environments and communities. Nevertheless, such women initiated significant, if subtle, transformations to lives and landscapes in the Old Town, offering a model of welfare practice which still has resonance today.

Figures 1 and 2 (as well as 5) show the children of St Saviour's Child Garden (SSCG) in its second home at 8 Chessel's Court. Opened in November 1906, this kindergarten was the outcome, in microcosm, of the very particular confluence of contemporary anxieties about the lives of the urban poor, especially children, with late Victorian social theory and feminist ideology, all of which were embodied in the work and life of its founder, Lileen Hardy, the woman the children watch so closely as they play.

Like so many women reformers before and after her, Hardy did not seek personal glory and left no papers; she is not knowable in the way that a Geddes or a Littlejohn is. So we must come to her obliquely, through official records and the documentation that survives of the kindergarten itself. Thus we find her first in Census records in the place of her birth, Salisbury. Born in 1872, she was one of the six children of a chemist. By 1901, and described as a kindergarten teacher and governess, she was resident in Edinburgh, working for a family in Charlotte Square. She was, then, one of a relatively new type of woman: a daughter of the middle classes who wanted, and likely needed, to work, and who, thanks to the opening up of education to girls by mid-century feminists, could receive a decent education and even entertain thoughts of a career.

Friedrich Froebel's concept of the kindergarten (and its development by his followers) was at the forefront of progressive thinking about education at this date. It appealed to reform-minded Victorians and Edwardians as they sought to turn away from the rigidity of contemporary social codes. As Hardy herself wrote:

> 'The kindergarten discards the abstract learning and instruction which have no relation to the child's physical, mental or spiritual needs, and places him instead in a little world of action where he can develop his personality along the lines of his own natural activities, his social life by contact with his peers. In childhood there is only one true means of real self-expression, and that is play. Organised play, is, in the child-stage – work!'

Integral to the successful practice of the kindergarten method were, in Froebel's mind, trained women teachers. They did not need to be mothers; indeed, by virtue of their training they could out-nurture those who had actually given birth. He thereby opened up a significant area of work for middle-class single women but, importantly, one which did not transgress their femininity. Hardy, in an appeal for a co-worker, written in 1907, explained:

> 'To be a kindergartner is the perfect development of womanliness – a working with God at the very fountain of artistic and intellectual power and moral character. It is therefore the highest finish that can be given to a woman's education to be trained for a kindergartner.'

Hardy was among the first students at the Sesame House for Home-Life Training, in London. This had been established in 1899 by members of the Sesame Club, an association for those interested in what were described as the 'new principles' of literature, art and education. Sesame House served in part as a finishing school, intended 'to fit girls and women more fully for the woman's life' through the acquisition of housekeeping skills but it had as its 'secondary purpose the preparing of girls who need to earn their livelihood as certificated lady nurses to children, as kindergarten teachers, and as nursery governesses.' Teaching was, naturally, on Froebelian lines; the head and her assistant being 'imported' from Pestalozzi-Froebel Haus in Berlin.

In the large house on Acacia Avenue, St John's Wood, Hardy entered a 'world of action' for young women, following a curriculum which encompassed, as a journalist reported, 'the theory and practice of education, child-development, natural science, hygiene and general household management.' This learning through doing also extended to the unique feature of Sesame House, its Free Kindergarten. This was an initiative to expand the benefits of the kindergarten method from the middle classes to the children of the working classes. For, at the same time as Froebel's ideas chimed with contemporary ideals of womanliness, his emphasis on child nurture and self-realization offered one way to address contemporary concerns about the state of the nation and its people.

At their root was the growing awareness that Britain no longer enjoyed the industrial and imperial dominance it had built up since the eighteenth century: competitor states such as Germany and Japan were increasingly powerful and, as time would tell, bellicose. At the same time, the possibility of the nation being able to maintain, at the very least, its world status, seemed ever more under threat as a new wave of detailed social research revealed the abject state of health of its workers. In Edinburgh statistics showed that death rates in the Old Town were twice that of the New (the population of the Canongate was an overcrowded 40, 000). If Britain were to progress, changes needed to be wrought on the bodies and environments of the urban poor.

For advocates of the Free Kindergarten, as Hardy, by virtue of her training, became, the starting point for reform lay with society's youngest members. She wrote: '...everyone who is thinking about the problems of poverty and degradation will acknowledge that no other method can compare with that of striking at their root in the children of today who will be the men and women of tomorrow.' Slum conditions, Free Kindergartners argued, stifled the children's true instincts, especially when they were at an age 'when the instinct for activity and industry is strong.' No society could continue to prosper if this were the case. The solution was to do what Hardy planned: to create the transforming environment of a kindergarten within the slums themselves. There, instead of being banished to wander the streets, or be watched over by a disgruntled older sister who should have been at school, young children could daily embark on a morning of activity which was designed to enable them to realize their potential to contribute fully to society.

It took Hardy five years to realize in the SSCG what she called 'the great desire of my heart'. In the meantime she had to earn a living. Her great fortune, and a key influence on the form her kindergarten took, was to have found employment with a very particular Edinburgh family, the Whytes, at number seven Charlotte Square.

Jane Whyte was a prominent member of Edinburgh's progressive circles;

her husband, The Reverend Alexander Whyte, was well-known in his day as a theologian, academic and minister of Free St George's Church, Shandwick Place. Since the early 1880s she had been associated with the Secular Positivist group that met in the nearby home of James and Edith Oliphant (whose sister Anna was married to Patrick Geddes). Among its concerns was the improvement of the quality of life of the poor in Edinburgh, and it was from this group that emerged, under Geddes's aegis (though not for long his direction) the Edinburgh Social Union. Largely run by women, Whyte was a founder member, and it was she, with her brother, who in 1887, purchased Whitehorse Close, one of the first properties that the Union renovated and ran as model social housing.

It seems unlikely that Hardy was unaware of Whyte's endeavours, and it surely led her to make her own way to the Old Town. Some time in 1905 or 1906 she attended a service at the Episcopalian church of Old St Paul's (OSP). Since the early 1890s the church had developed a programme of social work in the slums that formed its hinterland, which aimed at transforming the lives (inner and outer) of the poor, gaining a new impetus with the appointment as its rector in 1897 of the charismatic Albert Laurie. By 1902, this work comprised a women's settlement, which ran a team of women district visitors, and housed in the former type foundry at Whitefoord House, there were club rooms, a gymnasium, and a dispensary which offered affordable medical care.

Hardy saw an opportunity, and proposed to Laurie that she open a kindergarten under the church's auspices. He had long been interested in child welfare and education and the addition of some sort of educational facility to its programme would place OSP (and the Episcopal church) at the forefront of welfare provision in the Old Town. After much debate and discussion about whether a school or kindergarten would be better, Hardy prevailed and it was agreed that she could establish the SSCG at the OSP's mission hall (St Saviour's, hence the kindergarten's name) in Brown's Close. It was opened on All Saint's Day, 1906 (Figure 3).

Into the panelled mission room were brought tables and chairs; the walls adorned with appropriate pictures. A curtain of Liberty fabric (made by Hardy,

3 Interior of the St Saviour's Child Garden ca. autumn 1907 (courtesy OSP Archive)
4 Lileen Hardy, Canon Laurie and the Children at work in the garden at Brown's Close (courtesy OSP Archive)

5 The Children in the Garden at Chessel's Court with Canon Laurie (courtesy of the City of Edinburgh, Museum of Childhood)

the modernity of her taste signified by its manufacturer) divided the space in two, closing off the hall's altar. Clean, well-lit and ventilated, it was at once a very different space from the one-roomed dwellings in which most of her charges dwelt, and a familiar one, housed, as it was within a dilapidated pair of old cottages and situated at the end of a narrow close. It embodied, therefore, the sort of transformation that the children would themselves undergo as they were exposed to the new influences and values of kindergarten.

Marking their transposition into this new environment, the children began each day by donning a smock (blue with a red/pink collar and cuffs) and, once called to order, sang a greeting song to one another. Next came some marching or running, then the more serious 'work' began in making the room a fit space for play. They watered the potted plants, brought fresh seed to their canary, dusted the furniture and made the dolls' beds, later taking turns to act as 'monitor' and distribute food at break time. By the spring of 1907, a patch of wasteland attached to the hall was cleared and, with advice from Patrick Geddes himself (surely via Jane Whyte), was laid out. This served both for play but also as a site where the children could learn to cultivate plants to their potential as they were being nurtured by Hardy herself, (Figure 4).

Although Hardy initially ran the kindergarten largely on her own, she soon benefitted from the wave of women-originated and women-centred work developing alongside her venture in the Old Town. OSP's team of district visitors identified potential children for the SSCG (after Laurie had selected the first dozen or so pupils) and persuaded mothers to let them attend, while from its dispensary came nurses to look after the children. Hardy lived in their hostel at Plainstone's Close before moving in 1908 to Chessel's Court. The city's Medical Women were also valuable allies. Inheritors of the mantel of the Edinburgh Seven, they were tireless workers up and down the Royal Mile. Chief among them was Dr Isabel Venters, 'the lady wi the reid heid', as locals called her, who was the surgeon to the OSP's dispensary and became the SSCG's medical inspector. Important too were the young women who worked with Hardy as fellow kindergartners and the wealthy ladies in the New Town who donated money for her work.

That we know this much about the kindergarten, and have photographs of the children at 'work', is thanks to Hardy's careful documentation of her heart's desire from its beginning. The progressive nature of the Free Kindergarten (in 1906 there were no more than five in the British Isles) meant that its advocates had to work hard to propagandize its benefits for society. Hardy also needed to cultivate support for her work in its early days. Her first 'publications' were a series of handwritten letters describing the daily life of the kindergarten and particular events. These were distributed to interested parties and served to elicit gifts of equipment and teaching assistance. The need for directly financial support became more acute as the kindergarten entered its third year. Until this point Hardy had, by dint of careful saving while a governess, provided most of the funding. Now it was clear that it was doing good work – district visitors reported how popular an institution it was among Canongate mothers – it needed a more secure financial basis.

In 1908, therefore, Hardy initiated a more concerted fundraising campaign producing a foolscap pamphlet, The Life of a Slum Child. Complete with suitably dreary photographs, this documented a slum child's first years and showed how she might be transformed by the kindergarten. Its distribution seems to have encouraged benefactors to support the move, in September 1908, to the larger premises at 8, Chessel's Court, and its conversion into a suitably transformative environment. This had six rooms as well as a large rear garden (subsequently augmented by a second) and allowed Hardy to begin teaching her older children the 3Rs, and to schedule much more activity in the open air (Figure 5). In 1912, when funds were again tight, Hardy turned the round letters into a book, the Diary of a Free Kindergarten

In writing the Diary, Hardy's intention was to gain support for the SSCG, whether financial or in kind. As such, the facts and images she included were intended as persuasive devices to elicit sympathy in her readers. In some respects, then, we might understand it as a work of fiction. Nevertheless it is possible to use it to build a basic outline of the kindergarten's history and, whatever Hardy may have intended, to glean from it unintended information: a sense of what it was like to be a young middle-class reformer in the Edinburgh slums, and the characters of the children and their families who were the objects of her work.

Hardy comes across as a serious and devout young woman. Like so many of her generation she felt that the privileges she had enjoyed as an educated middle-class woman required of her a career of service, working to better the lives of her working-class sisters and their children. That such work was also liberating – allowing her to live alone (albeit with a housekeeper) and move beyond class boundaries – is clear. Describing a working party formed of herself, and assorted fathers, brothers, and mothers of the children, to prepare the new garden at Brown's Close she wrote: 'There is a delightful naturalness in our personal relations all working together. To exchange tools with a man and take a turn at his job gives a pleasant intimacy which nothing else brings.'

That hers might have been a sometimes solitary existence also comes across. Following the move to Chessel's Court, and another working party (there were many), one of the mothers inspected her new quarters. Admiring its simplicity – 'If ye put onything mair in it ye would spile it.' She added 'it must be lonesome for ye. If ye only had some yin to come in nights, to share your bed.'

Building a relationship with the mothers was core to the Free Kindergarten project. As Hardy wrote, 'She who takes the child by the hand takes the mother by the heart.' The benefits of better manners, cleaner habits and sociability that the environment of the SSCG brought to the children – which the mothers soon acknowledged – would, it was anticipated, encourage them to effect changes in their homes, in turn improving conditions for all the family. The relationship was clearly a good one. In June 1908 the mothers invited Hardy and other kindergarten workers to a picnic at Cramond. Subsequently they created a Mother's Guild with the aim of co-operation between school and home; its rules included putting the children to bed 'at a fixed early hour'. A collective gift of a new offertory table (Laurie visited weekly to conduct prayers), Hardy noted, brought a lump to her throat. While the sight of a mother, who had given birth only two weeks previously, scrubbing a poorly neighbour's floor, made her muse on the fuss she had made over a recent illness, writing 'It is not only Crimean Wars that make Florence Nightingales. Commonplace everyday life creates many heroines in the Canongate.'

And what of the children? The poverty of their living conditions was a constant theme in Hardy's account. She noted how, when her first three pupils arrived at the mission hall, they assumed it was her home because, like theirs, it was one room with a partition. Later on, she recorded watching them create a tenement from the middle-class architecture of a donated doll's house, and quoted them: 'this is my hoose, that's your hoose, that's Peggie's hoose.'

The challenges of language were another theme, a shorthand for the initial divide between the middle-class Englishwoman and her high-spirited Scots-speaking charges. Initially, they had difficulty with her name, settling, at first, for 'the wumman' and then 'the wumman' with the apology, 'I'm aye forgetting your name.' They were mystified when asked to sweep the floor, thinking she meant flowers rather than the 'flair' (these are Hardy's transliterations). Gradually Hardy learnt their language, realizing that 'what's the matter' was better substituted by 'what's wrang wi' ye.' Such adaptations on her part signal what becomes clearer as the Diary progresses: the sense that mutual incomprehension gave way to a growing sense of working together in a shared venture.

The first cohort of children left in 1911, moving on to the care of 'the model slum headmaster', Andrew Young, at the New Street School. Their teacher reported proficiency in class work, four ranking among the best in class, and their very good manners, writing 'They are most amenable, very mannerly, kindly natured, and truthful always'. These were the first of many 'graduates', for the SSCG long outlasted the lives of its founders. It was only in 1977, by which date the slums were gone and people had, perhaps, forgotten the imperative behind it, that it was closed. Nevertheless, today concerns for child welfare persist. And while there is much that we might find patronizing in the SSCG, Hardy's model of working within existing communities, of getting to know parents and building relationships between school and home, and of trained teachers using a child-centred (rather than outcome-focused) approach to early-years education, might yet be a benchmark for future progress.

LATTICING, HEXAGONS AND ENCHANTERS

TOM HUBBARD

1

At the beginning of March 2015, I visited Summerhall, the Edinburgh-based arts complex founded by Robert McDowell and Richard Demarco in the former Dick Veterinary School. The spring season was in prospect: the Scotland-Russia Forum was offering programmes in Russian language and culture (it's fitting that it is now based in the same building as the Demarco European Art Foundation, which engages with the contemporary arts of east and central Europe). The Scottish Community Drama's National Script Library is also based there; the building was the Edinburgh venue for a piece by a Gaelic theatre company; and in April there would be the third Summerhall Historical Fiction Festival, hosted by Allan Massie and Iain Gale.

Summerhall is the nucleus of what has become known as a Free University – not 'free' in the sense that you don't have to pay – professionals need fees – but insofar as its programmes are open to all. That is a cardinal principle of the Free University movement, of which Robert McDowell has been a major proponent for more than forty years.

2

My introduction to Free University concepts in Scotland – though it took me some time to recognise them as such – came during the late 1980s and early 1990s, when I was Librarian at the Scottish Poetry Library, then based in Tweeddale Court. Across the road from us was the Netherbow theatre (the future Scottish Storytelling Centre, under the stewardship of Donald Smith). Round the corner, in Blackfriars Street, Richard Demarco and his colleagues filled a former kirk with arts events. This part of Edinburgh's Old Town, derelict in the 1970s, seemed to be coming alive. The cluster of venues was an attempted Free University, if not in name. These arts structures had an intellectual as well as a physical proximity. This was in just one pocket of Edinburgh that I happened to know, but not dissimilar energies were building elsewhere in the city, in other parts of Scotland and beyond.

At that time the composer Ronald Stevenson was giving lecture-recitals at the Scottish Poetry Library and the Demarco Gallery, and we spoke of his musical mentor, Ferruccio Busoni. The hero of Busoni's *Doktor Faust* represented the tragic side of humanity's quest for universality (embracing – as Faust puts it – north, south, west, and east); it was another Busoni opera, *Arlecchino*, which focused on the comic side of that quest. Arlecchino was the Italian *commedia dell'arte* figure who was the rougher version of elegant Frenchified Harlequin. The motley patches of Arlecchino's costume suggested a multi-faceted personality, a Latin lightness as counterpart to Faust's darkness. We needed both.

Independently of all this, in 1990, the Scottish Poetry Library's director, Tessa Ransford, gave a lecture at Tübingen University where she offered an image akin to Arlecchino's lozenges: 'In mathematics there is a concept known as "latticing" which gives a layered, multi-dimensional ordering of events or elements. Lattices are a graphic demonstration of the quantum postulate that there is always at least one alternative between every this and every that. They are like flow-charts, based on the uncertainly principle.' Ransford then went on to celebrate the work of the Scottish philosopher George Davie, whose books on 'the democratic intellect' and the Scottish tradition of generalism in education were finding a new readership.

In 1991 the art critic Murdo Macdonald joined forces with Tessa, myself, the sculptor Kenny Munro and others in an exploration of the writings of Patrick Geddes who, a century earlier, had been instrumental in reviving the cultural life of the Old Town. Meanwhile, Richard Demarco – with the cooperation of Robert McDowell – was developing his own projects along the lines of his friend and co-conspirator of the 1970s, the German avant-garde artist Joseph Beuys. It became clear that the philosophies of Geddes and Beuys, pioneers respectively of the 'democratic intellect' and of the Free International University movement, were – to use a musical term favoured by Ronald Stevenson – enharmonic.

3

Patrick Geddes grew up in Perth. He developed his passions for botany and geology on Kinnoull Hill, effectively the first of the many 'Outlook Towers' he inaugurated throughout his life. The Edinburgh one is situated between the Lawnmarket and the Castle; in Geddes's day it was a people's palace of education. From its top, one could visually connect various intellectual disciplines - for example, the courts (law) and the Salisbury Crags (geology). In 1904 Geddes proposed to the Carnegie Dunfermline Trust what might be called a more-than-university, located in the former capital. Drawing on the Scandinavian innovation of open-air (and open-access) museums, Geddes aimed to transform Dunfermline's Pittencrieff Park into the locus of a daringly wide range of educational attractions that would appeal to children as well as to adults.

Geddes's generalist counter to specialisation was not altogether welcome to conventional academics, who objected to a botanist presuming to step beyond his own discipline. Hugh MacDiarmid, quoting the man himself, remarked that 'Geddes's constant effort "was to help people to think for themselves, not in scraps and bits". He knew that watertight compartments are useful only to a sinking ship, and traversed all the boundaries of separate subjects.' In addition to generalism, however, Geddes had a second criterion for what would become the Free University movement, and this was noted by MacDiarmid: 'The reawakening of the vital and the organic in every department undermines the authority of the purely mechanical.' Exaltation of the organic over the mechanical has a long pedigree in Victorian Scotland and England in the writings of Carlyle and Ruskin. And in Germany there was the *Lebensphilosophie* of Rudolf Steiner, whose tenets are traceable back to Goethe and Schiller, who in turn influenced Carlyle. It is on this German line of intellectual genealogy that we find Joseph Beuys, whose impact on the thinking and practice of Summerhall's Robert McDowell and Richard Demarco cannot be exaggerated.

4

As a Luftwaffe pilot in 1941, Beuys was shot down over Crimea, survived, and was cared for by Tatars who covered him with felt and fat, and fed him with honey and horses' milk. He went on to become a professor at the Düsseldorf Academy of Art, but was sacked for allowing anyone and everyone into his lecture halls to receive his unconventional teaching. During his first working trip to Scotland, at the invitation of Demarco, in 1970, Beuys declared: 'I see the land of Macbeth'. A few years later, Beuys was back in Edinburgh, collaborating with Demarco and the Polish theatre director Tadeusz Kantor in the Poorhouse, off Forrest Road.

When he was accused of talking 'about everything under the sun, except art', Beuys replied 'Everything under the sun is art'. The Free International University (FIU) for Creativity and Interdisciplinary Research, which he co-founded with the novelist Heinrich Böll, was intended as an alternative to established institutions. 'In places like universities,' Beuys wrote, 'where everyone talks so rationally, it is necessary for a kind of enchanter to appear.' When one reads the manifesto of the FIU one can imagine the shade of Patrick Geddes nodding sagely: 'Whereas the specialist's insulated point of view places the arts and other kinds of work in sharp opposition, it is in fact crucial that the structural, formal and thematic problems of the various work processes should be constantly compared with one another.' In the course of a 1977 interview, Beuys expanded on the *raison d'être* of the FIU – the abiding motifs of his discussion were interconnectedness and organic process.

A year or so earlier, Caroline Tisdall and Robert McDowell, in the wake of Beuys's lecturing and exhibition work in Ireland, wrote up a study addressed to the EEC on the founding of the FIU in that country (German counter-culturalists found inspiration in the 'hedge schools' which had sprung up in defiance of the suppression of Irish culture). Beuys had wanted a physical building for the Irish FIU, but despite strong allies such as the future president Mary Robinson, the Dublin proposal fell through.

The Tisdall/McDowell report contains this, which echoes Beuys himself: 'The logical consequence of the current sense of change in Ireland is an increased interest in the comparison of ideas from outside. This matches the particular soft spot that many feel for Ireland, and the position it occupies in the imagination and cultural heritage of Europe. The Free University would hope to bring such concerns in Ireland into contact with interests from outside, the aim being to compare ideas and thus create a dialogue which would register more effectively the affections, respect and concern that is felt for Ireland in many quarters [...] Ireland's resistance to standardisation, particularly in culture, is an important example for Europe ... Pride in Gaelic culture is one kind of buffer against standardisation. But it should be matched with an equally active assessment of contemporary culture.'

Without for one moment denying the claims of a sister country, if one reads 'Scotland' for 'Ireland' in the above, there are in 2015 special resonances on this side of the North Channel, and Summerhall is going a long way towards a Free International University in Scotland. In order both to secure and widen an FIUS, Summerhall needs allies beyond its walls.

In January 1985, a year before his death, in an interview with the French journal *Kanal,* Beuys said that man 'fragmented' was only too easily controllable by the state and other authoritarian institutions, religious, cultural and pedagogic. His strategy for achieving wholeness was summed up symbolically in the interlocking – latticing? – basalt hexagons of the Giant's Causeway, where he loved to stride. His key concept was 'invisible sculpture' or 'social sculpture', a higher form of networking of folk from diverse fields, who would not otherwise meet: this could require as much artistry as the creation of an 'art work', which only too often can be reified and fetishised as a commodity.

5

In the years following Beuys's death from heart failure in January 1986, the artist and activist James Marriott visited existing FIU structures in Germany and decided to set up an itinerant university that would meet in college spaces or in people's homes; this found bases in Glasgow, Sheffield, Bristol and London. It doesn't appear to have had a formal name, but it was clearly a precursor of PLATFORM, whose remit is 'art, education, social and environmental justice' and in which Mr Marriott is a prominent figure. Caroline Tisdall continued to be active and Shelley Sacks directed a Social Sculpture Research Unit at Oxford Brookes University.

I have mentioned what seemed to me to be FIU-like activity at this time in Edinburgh, but there was no little ferment in Glasgow during the late 1980s / early 1990s, and it was there that James Kelman and Peter Kravitz were active in a Free University - named as such. Its proposal included the following: 'The activities and projects of the organisation will be based on the exploration of different forms of learning, not centred on a teacher/pupil relationship but rather on group activity, the defence of ideas and the value of individual knowledge and skills.' At this time, east European dissident politics were articulating – in word and deed - the need to re-invigorate civil society, challenging a one-party monopoly of power. This found an echo in those struggling against the complacent domination by the Labour Party of the city of Glasgow. Peter Kravitz has also drawn my attention to the Free University Network (FUN), whose documents are deposited as part of the Spirit of Revolt 'archive of dissent' in Glasgow's Mitchell Library.

In more recent years, as part of the Ragged Project, free 'ragged' universities have been operating in Glasgow and Edinburgh. During 2011, the Glasgow one was advertising a wide range of classes, including courses on the immune system, women and dance, a discussion for parents on 'active storytelling', twentieth-century jazz, and – aptly – a talk on Robert Tressell, author of the influential working-class novel *The Ragged-Trousered Philanthropists*. This event marked the centenary of Tressell's untimely death. At Edinburgh, the Ragged University has hosted sessions on bringing up a bilingual child, 3-D printing, and a talk by Richard Gunn and Murdo Macdonald celebrating a new edition of George Davie's *The Democratic Intellect*. There is a healthy mix of group-generated activities and presentations by professionals. The Ragged Project website records the work of Colin Kirkwood, who was inspired by the writings of the Brazilian educationalist and philosopher Paulo Freire, and who was behind the Adult Learning Project based in the Gorgie/Dalry area of Edinburgh. I attended this during the late 1980s, as one learner among others; these sessions concerned the nature of literature, and as I remember they were readers', rather than writers', workshops.

The Free University movement can be said to owe some of its impetus to the work of the 'official' universities' centres of continuing education. In the course of his non-fictional writings from this time, James Kelman paid tribute to Philip Hobsbaum, whose class at Glasgow University nurtured Alasdair Gray and Tom Leonard – both of whom were involved in the Free University of Glasgow in the Eighties and Nineties - and Kelman himself. For a young working-class Leonard, public libraries had a similar ethos. At the Pollok branch library he discovered a wide range of literature: 'When the hero of *Crime and Punishment* ran down the stairs of a close after the murder, I knew what it was he ran down.' However, when Gray, Leonard and Kelman found themselves sharing a creative writing professorship at Glasgow University, they fell foul of the institution's apparatchiks, who opposed meaningful contact with students: as Gray recalled, 'we had taken professoring too seriously for a modern university.'

The Free University movement prioritises knowledge for its own sake rather than for qualifications or status. However, people still seek qualifications for honourably practical purposes, requiring accredited lecturers, assessment, risking attendant bureaucracy and form-filling with the apparent need to distinguish 'aims' from 'objectives'. Never too far away is the miasma of mission statements, straplines, happy-clappy guff-clouds predictably heralded by present participles ('creating opportunity', 'investing in people', etc.). Moreover, we must ask how far a Free University is a Free *International* University in the Beuysian sense, with sound lines of communication between the local and the universal, such as Tisdall and McDowell stressed in their Dublin proposals.

Christopher Harvie, a frequenter of Summerhall, has written of the 'small platoons' who nurture intellectual and creative culture in parsimonious times. Having cited Scottish examples of these, I'm only too aware of many I haven't mentioned. Their websites fairly sparkle with defiance and cheek. The Free University of Brighton meets in a variety of spaces including 'caravans and bandstands'; the revived Copenhagen Free University, earlier outlawed by the Danish Government (which prohibited the use of the term 'university' by unauthorised bodies), foregathers in a member's flat and declares: 'We call for everybody to establish their own free universities in their homes or in the workplace, in the square or in the wilderness. All power to the free universities of the future.' In the past, community groups, wary of bureaucracy, risked 'the tyranny of structurelessness'. However, the internet has increased possibility and effectiveness in ways that Beuys could never have envisaged.

Concluding a 2013 piece in the *London Review of Books*, the literary critic and historian of ideas Stefan Collini lamented that, in the wake of marketization, 'first-rate universities have become third-rate companies'. More recently, and in the same periodical, the art historian Marina Warner sharply criticised the UK university system, from which she – for all her eminence – has endured the run-around. 'Faith in the value of a humanist education', she remarked, 'is beginning to look like an antique romance.' She mocked the authoritarian jargon of campus management as 'a catechism for robots'.

All the more reason for a federation of existing and potential structures that follow the criteria of the Free International University movement; may they recognise themselves as such, find strength through numbers, and create a 'labyrinth of linkages' (Tolstoy) across Scotland. Summerhall is a centre for many but by no means all of these energies, but let them come together there via the web and in person. Let us use Summerhall as the base-camp for a Free International University of Scotland.

With thanks to Seán Bradley, Peter Kravitz and Todd McEwen for their guidance.

FURTHER READING Gray, Alasdair. *A Life in Pictures*, 2010. | Kelman, James. *Some Recent Attacks: Essays Cultural and Political*, 1991. | Leonard, Tom. Introduction to his anthology *Radical Renfrew*, 1990. | MacDiarmid, Hugh. *The Company I've Kept*, 1966 (on Patrick Geddes). | Miller, Mitch, and Johnny Rodger, *The Red Cockatoo*, 2011 (on Kelman's activism). | Rainbird, Seán. *Joseph Beuys and the Celtic World*, 2005.

OUTSIDE: INSIDE

••••••••◆◆◆◆◆◆◆◆◆◆••••••••

PAUL FURNEAUX

I was born in Ellon, and studied drawing and painting at the Edinburgh College of Art from 1982 to 1987. Eventually I moved to Tokyo, where I took up a place at Tama Art University on the masters course studying traditional and contemporary techniques in Japanese woodcut printing. I was awarded the prestigious Monbusho scholarship from 1996 to 2000. I completed my studies and returned home the same year, taking up a post as artist in residence at the Royal Museum of Scotland as part of the nationwide Year of the Artist programme.

I had a studio for ten years in the Cowgate. It burned down during the large fire there in December 2002 which engulfed around 20 buildings. There were grand plans to include space for artists in the redevelopment of that area, but in my experience that's something that's always expendable, and it never happened. Fortunately I was able to relocate to Stockbridge at WASPS Patriothall studios, where I have now been for about ten years.

The main focus of my work continues to be in Mokuhanga (the Japanese term for woodcut print). I use ancient techniques of cutting wood with a variety of knives and gouges. The wood is then dampened, watercolor is applied to the cut wood with specialist printing brushes. Using Japanese paper the image is printed by hand with the aid of a baren, a saucer-sized disc wrapped in bamboo leaf.

I have exhibited my work nationally and internationally. My recent works have a pared-down visual language, which highlights the inherent beauty of my chosen medium. Recently I've developed a technique where some of the prints are wrapped around found and made sculptural objects. This has given the works not only a character of their own, but also a dimension which can further be explored - a shifting passage between pictorial and physical space. This autumn I will have a solo exhibition in London for the first time since my old studio was destroyed.

Paul Furneaux's Outside: Inside, A Contemporary Use of Japanese Woodcut Printing is at the William Road Gallery, NW1, from 23 October to 13 November.

LETTER FROM BARCELONA

BRIAN McLAUGHLIN

A tourist is something I have never wanted to be, especially in the capital of my country. A traveller takes a journey of discovery; a tourist leaves the nine-to-five self at home and tries on someone else's shoes for a couple of weeks, eating not *too* exotic food at slightly different times, parroting half-understood phrases to patient hotel and shop staff, bringing back ill-chosen souvenirs to remind himself and his friends of that other place, that other, carefree him or her. A traveller is always himself, even when hurtling through space and time. From an early age I realised that if I could not write like Stevenson, I could travel like him, if I could not sing or play guitar like James Taylor, I could hitch-hike and feel heroically melancholy and brave and misunderstood.

These were the feelings this thirty-one-year-old traveller took with him to Barcelona in 1986, after time spent in France and India. I arrived at 2.00 am on the 24th of September, with only pounds and francs in my pocket. Crowds of people were streaming back past me like extras from the Night of the Walking Dead, as I trundled my luggage downtown from the Eurolines bus stop to an address near the Picasso Museum. With impeccable timing, I had arrived at the end of the city's annual celebration, its *Festa Major*, with a charge to find a job and an apartment in a week, or go on to another adventure, in Venice. I had an address and a name of a girl I had never met. I spoke no Spanish nor what I assumed was the local dialect, Catalan. When I found the address, I was confronted with a series of nameless door buzzers. In Spain, I found out, people do not post their names with their door number. I looked around to see two wiry young men, calmly prising car doors open then stealing their radios and anything of value they could find. I thought of the cash I had on me, all my savings. Luckily a neighbour from the adjoining stair came by, asked me in English what I was doing there and somehow used his key to let me in the main door. I found the apartment. The girl's mother was visiting from England and refused to let me in. No matter, I slumped on the doorstep and happily snoozed until Petra showed up as the sun was rising.

I found a job and a flat in the city's old town. And I stayed in Barcelona for the next thirty years, running a business, studying and teaching. My two children were born here and both my sisters still live not far from my first flat. The best accounts in English of what Barcelona was like in that fertile period between the washed grey immediate post-Franco years and the 1992 Olympic bloom, can be found in the writings of Giles Tremlett and of Colm Tóibín. Tremlett laments the loss of the edginess, of the thrilling menace of the Barrio Chino, the seedy bars off the Ramblas, the prostitutes wearing fur coats and nothing else on the Rambla de Catalunya. Tóibín talks about the reaffirmation of Catalan identity and remembers the paella restaurants perched on the scrap of beach in the Barceloneta district, an old fisherman's quarter, which were demolished, like so many other things, to make way for the new Olympic city and the twenty-five miles of new beaches created then. 'Barcelona lives with its back to the sea' was a local saying. It was true. I had been there for six weeks before I realised that behind some warehouses about five hundred yards away from where I lived in the Carrer Princesa, lay the Mediterranean. In 1992, however, Barcelona followed the example of Boston and turned itself around to face the water. It was the single most important act in the dramatically successful transformation of the city, marking out its difference with Madrid and attracting a whole new range of tourists and hotel and restaurant developments. A new ring road was also built, temporarily easing the traffic pressure in the city centre, the rail tracks were torn up and the shiny new trains redirected from the coast to the centre of town, then trams were installed and work began on a new nearly 48 kilometre long extension to the Metro. Planned for 2008, it is still unfinished, with tracks deserted, and many of its stations mothballed.

These last two projects, along with the new skyscrapers, were the slightly rotten fruit of the 'Forum of the Cultures'. If, despite some caveats, the 1992 Olympics can be said to have been an almost magical enthronement of the power of imaginative city planning, the problem of using an important event to fire change is that there are not always suitable events available.

In 1994, when asked what would be the next catalytic event, the Mayor replied that they would host the World's Fair in 2004. When it was pointed out that there was no Fair scheduled in that year, he retorted that Barcelona would create the Forum of Cultures. And it did, in the process extending the new buildings past the Olympic Village, building a huge new marina, several public exhibition spaces and for the first time an area of high-rise buildings later used to attract budding silicon valley types with urbane urban chic. The 22@ district, as it came to be known, would be part of Catalonia's effort to be the European Massachusetts, the President of the Regional Government declared. Its architecture reflects this dream.

Barcelona's love affair with ambitious town planning and architecture is well-known and not always positive. In the 90s, the socialist Mayor declared that the city needed a building by Richard Meier, so he commissioned the architect to build a showpiece Museum of Contemporary Art, despite the fact that Barcelona had no real collection of contemporary art. The building is like a slab of vanilla ice cream dropped on the pavement. Perhaps its biggest contribution to city culture is the use of its steps by the Old Town's skateboarders.

Buildings are not designed only for function or beauty however: architecture is political, especially in Barcelona. The modern projects were fostered by the Socialists to show how cosmopolitan they are, to highlight their differences with the nationalist parties, who in turn favour solid, even clunky anachronistic projects such as the re-erection of the four Greek columns representing the four bands of the Catalan flag in the Plaça de Espanya, the Rodinesque work of the sculptor Clarés or the unending staircase on top of a Catalunya-shaped stone block in Placa Catalunya commemorating the pre-civil war President, Francesc Macià. The latter was the work of their favourite contemporary sculptor, the recently deceased Josep Maria Subirachs. He was commissioned to execute the work on the Passion Façade of the Sagrada Familia, which he carried out with few concessions to Gaudi's original style. I used to observe him eating lunch at the next table several times a week in the early nineties. He was a hard-working, unassuming man with straggly grey hair and surprisingly small hands who ate alone, bent over his newspaper resting on the white paper tablecloth, while the waiter slapped down the dish of *butifarra i mongetes*. Perhaps he, like me, had chosen the Restaurant Bilbao more for its address at the intersection of Venus and Danger Streets than for its food. Perhaps he too was a traveller in Barcelona.

My favourite modern Catalan architect, the late Enric Miralles, links Barcelona to the Edinburgh Old Town, not just because his studio designed the Scottish Parliament with all of the daring inspiration and quirky design motifs of the Barcelona school, but because, as I discovered when I went to see his recent remodelling of the Santa Caterina market in the Barcelona old town, its façade is covered by some startlingly familiar wooden staves! In each case, the fit with the local environment was one of the justifications of the aesthetic choice made by the architect. Barcelona has 39 municipal markets, more than any other European city and has known how to invest in them, providing cash machines, basement supermarkets and car-parks to help them keep pace with changing shopping trends. The city also has the most restrictive opening hours in Spain to protect its thousands of small shops, although that policy is coming under increasing pressure and the new high rents which owners are able to charge mean many venerable city centre premises are being taken over by chains. La Mercat de Sant Josep- la Boqueria, the most famous market on the Ramblas, is sinking under the avalanche of tourists. Fruit stalls are being replaced by smoothie stands and cafés. It has had to limit groups of more than sixteen visitors to Fridays to allow local customers to get near the stalls. A difficult line between adaptation or death, and accommodation and extinction, is being walked.

How do you manage all these people? When I first lived in Barcelona, tourism was seasonal with a summer peak. Now it is year round. Around two and a half million cruise ship passengers now pass through Barcelona every year, and two or three times a year over 65,000 tourists arrive in a single weekend. They disembark onto concertina lines of waiting taxis and buses to be taken to the Sagrada Familia, and then on to the booming international luxury shops on the Passeig de Gracia, perhaps stopping for a glass of overpriced sangria on their way back to the boat. Their food and accommodation are already taken care of, so they spend relatively little in town. According to official figures, tourist numbers increased from just under two million in 1990, to almost eight million in 2014, for a city with a core population of under two million inhabitants. The new radical city council is trying to ban the construction of hotels and agrees with its predecessor's ban on unauthorised tourist apartments as well as cancelling plans for a luxury Russian-owned marina at the bottom of the Ramblas. They face a long judicial struggle, as many of the projects approved by previous hotel-friendly councils are locked in by complex contracts. They have had to backtrack already in areas such as Barceloneta, where their local voters had taken to the streets to complain about drunken tourists parading semi-naked, about their local shops turning into gift shops and restaurants becoming kebab outlets, premises acquired at astronomical rents whose subsequent low level of business makes people suspect them of being involved in money-laundering activities.

People also understand the importance of the tourist industry to the local economy, especially during the crisis. The letters columns in the local papers are a to-and-fro between complaints about the tourist takeover of the city and fears that combatting it will damage the already weak economy. The real question may be not just about controlling the negative effects of so much tourism without killing the economy, but how to change the mind-set from one of perpetual growth to one of proposing a set of social, economic and cultural limits. The figures provided by the tourist authorities are generally historical. We know how many people have visited and can make projections for the near future. But do we know how many tourists we want to visit our city? Does Edinburgh know exactly how big it wants its Festivals to be? What would be the implications (for both cities) of the new Mayor Ada Colau's suggestion that Barcelona fixes the social and cultural model it wants then decides how much tourism can fit into that rather than the other way around?

And what does Barcelona mean to the visitors and why does that matter? The tourist shops on the Ramblas would suggest by their wares it means Mexican hats, bullfighting (now banned in Catalonia) and sangria (seldom drunk there). Once my children were born, we moved to a seaside town twenty-five minutes from the centre. The train line goes up the coast to Blanes and therefore it was common to have to stand on my commuter trip while the seats were taken up by rosy hued tourists. On the homeward journey I would often see the same people, happy and tired after their visit. Often upon chatting to them about their day, I would find they had got off at Sants Station, walked or taken a metro to Camp Nou and then come back to the train. For these people, Barcelona meant Barcelona Football Club. Its Museum comes ahead of the one devoted to Picasso in terms of visitors.

For Catalans too, Barcelona Football Club is a standard bearer of their identity. Josep Sunyol, one of the Club's presidents was shot by Franco's troops. Its stadium is technically sold out for every game to season-ticket holders made up of whole families, from granny to granddaughter, in remembrance of the days when it was the only place they could speak Catalan. Its slogan, *'Més que un club'* ('More than a Club') hints at its aspirations. And yet, and yet. Members routinely sell tickets for individual games with the help of the Club to visitors to the city and at a match you will often hear more Russian, Arabic, Chinese or French around you than Catalan. Due to global television agreements, matches are often played at nine or ten p.m., shutting out local schoolchildren and working people. For decades, the club refused sponsorship on the team's strips – now Qatar features prominently, with rumours flying that Camp Now may be rebaptised with its sponsor's name. What do people mean when they chant 'Barça' all over the world?

For the name and meaning of Barcelona has undergone significant shift in recent years, from RyanAir's rechristening of any airport within 100 kilometres of the city as Barcelona, to the local media's and the airport's use of the initials BCN , now in common use, although if you look the initials up on Wikipedia you will also be referred to a whole list of places, from lower California to the British Commonwealth of Nations, to a skyscraper in Frankfurt. This matters, because once you slowly blend your identity to suit the needs of the visitor, the big company, the tourist, you can lose it. This is particularly ironic in the case of Barcelona, the capital of a Catalonia which is striving to defend and reaffirm its identity and its own language. In a global marketplace, all those new signature architectural buildings risk making you just like everywhere else rather than marking you out as unique.

BCN World, 'designed as a meeting point between East and West and between America and Asia' according to its promoters, is a project currently underway, a new mini-Las Vegas with casinos, hotels and shopping outlets, benefitting from its own labour and tax laws and possibly side-stepping anti-smoking legislation. It is backed by the major Catalan bank, La Caixa, to be built on land its social and cultural foundation owns adjacent to a large amusement park. The home page on BCN World's website features the usual images of the Sagrada Familia and the new skyscrapers and refers to Barcelona as a 'multipurpose city' and a 'socioeconomic icon'. Only on the last page do we see that the development is located about 100 kilometres from Barcelona, just south of Tarragona. The Barcelona City council has tried to block the appropriation of the city's name, but to no avail.

Control of your own identity is important whether at an individual, city or country level. You surrender it at your peril. The Viking ceremonies at New Year certainly liven up Edinburgh, but are we perhaps borrowing another identity to please the tourist? There are Fringe Festivals all over the world now. Could the Edinburgh Festival just move to Manchester?

I am a creature of habit, even of ritual. Like Boswell, when I leave

Edinburgh I often go down to the foot of the High Street and look up at Arthur's Seat. We need to cling on to icons of identity lest the tourist in all of us totally takes over from the travelling citizen. In Barcelona, I step under the wooden staves into the Santa Caterina market, push past the tourists to listen to the eternal voice of the market woman asking me, 'Què vols, maco?'.

POEMS

KEN CRUMP

◆◆◆◆◆◆◆

JOYCE GUTHRIE

◆◆◆◆◆◆◆

NEIL YOUNG

FLOODLANDS OF THE DUCKABUSH

Upon the floodlands the Duckabush River
slows to a flow at dusk.
Moon pulls the sea inward and moves towards
the mountains – a pale silhouette iridescent.

'Reddish Face' – a native village place.
The name now a lost clouded image, like the craggy glacier
which birthed a tributary, that tumbles over eagle swooped cliffs
high upon vales; gives way to boulder tossed rales
before becoming a gentle meandered grass-covered backwash.

Upon the floodlands of the Duckabush
early night air awakes to the sound of red-winged blackbirds.
Deer graze frost topped grass near the edge
of the silent course where boughed limbs
of evergreen, with their long bent arms, tremble.

'Duck-a-boos' – mythical king of salmon, the Twana tribe claims,
gathered in small plateaus where the river collects in pools
as eddies swirl round stones and trunks of fallen tree forms.

Up past the floodlands,
the 'Duck' bends a way through forest and bush.
Rapids climb to squatted pines where roots
cling to boulders on elevated heights.

Escarpments rise red near the river
where crooked mouth salmon swim.
The walls of steep slopes fall to the wayside
of a smooth chute through which the river slides.

A force that roars echoes through the canyon
far above the tree line where muffled sounds
mumble words from tongues heard in ancient rhyme.

Do-he-a-bos, Do-hi-a-bos, Duc-a-bos
Names changed from ancient age.

Streams find a way to the river
One Too Many Creek
Crazy Creek
converge with the Duckabush where on a mountain
now the same name was once known as
Skookum, Arline, Susan.

From the shrouded mist peek the ancient spirits,
now tumbled silhouettes, which in moon lit rain
splatter sounds of
Do-he, do-hi, do-he, do-hi, Duc-a-bos.

Tears fall on the mouth of the floodlands
as the Duckabush River slows to a flow at dusk.

Ken Crump

FOOTFALL OR DEATH OF A TOURIST

We lost one today on Lothian Road,
father of five from Iowa, makes you think
about travel, the broad vistas it opens up,
what adventures, what departures from the daily norm.

Easy enough to do, slip from the kerb
before an authentic Number 2, my word how the locals
gasped as his rucksack rolled on the road,
it bore the legend 'Motherfucker, USA.'

We know this much, he was short stay,
cheap hop from Stansted, flying at a tangent
to his European tour. Never planned it, so
we never really got to know him.

The ambulance man scooped up the half-written
postcards fanned out on the tarmac, the Tartan shawl,
the Bobby statue made in Taiwan. (Surely
there's a procedure for dealing with unwanted souvenirs?)

We lost one today on Lothian Road
but be thankful, it was an unhappy accident, no one's fault.
His death was instant – and, he was heading west from here,
already among the counted in June's footfall.

Joyce Guthrie

THE LOCK-UP, 1969

On Saturday afternoons I'd turn up
Where once-blue doors were too warped to close
And the smell of oiled rags and scraped car rust
Transported me, incense-like at my nose.
Spanners, jump-leads, welding rods and pliers
Were the manly instruments of this domain
Where he would be stretched beneath the chassis,
Fag in, singing 'Mona Lisa' – again.

That Hillman Minx was remade by repairs
Though that was all part of the alchemy
For I got to hold tools, to pass them on
And then, at six, home time, and stew for tea,
I'd clamber between his knees in the seat
And steer, king of the road right down our street.

Neil Young

THE POCKETBOOK GUIDE TO SCOTTISH SUPERHEROES

KIRSTI WISHART

I felt it before I heard it. A wave of pressure easing me over to the side of the room, then the BOOM hit, gave the place a shake, the anger spilling out of me, 'Christ, not *tonight* - '

I flinched, checked to see if they'd woken Mum up. Because there'd have been hell to pay if they had, I'd have been *raging*. Bloody superheroes or not, I'd be phoning the police, making a complaint.

It had been a nightmare getting her to sleep, the drugs taking ages and now the daft wee glass ornaments on the dressing table were levitating, floating a good inch above where they should be, dancing about, the mirror rattling like it was having a laugh. The aftershock shoogling the air set off a buzzing in my chest and I coughed. But Mum, thankfully, was oblivious, snoring away.

Once I'd got breath back enough to sigh, the ornaments floating back to where they should be, everything settling, I risked tip-toeing to the curtains to check the all clear. But my timing was rubbish, a blaze of white blinding me. I pulled the curtain back quick but it didn't make much difference, the walls bright like there was a bloody great light-house outside our top floor flat.

A second later it was back to darkness and I was whispering '*Bastards*' when a band of green crept round the edges of the window, raced about the room, stopped a few inches on the headboard above Mum's head. Was it the Northern Lights maybe? Because from what I could remember The Fenian had been banned from Dundee airspace. Whoever it was, they were being a right nuisance and as I thought that the green vanished, left her alone.

Rubbed my eyes, tried to ease the sleep away. Mum's alarm clock read 1:06am. A school night as well. I figured the drugs would keep her quiet until about 5am as long as those idiots didn't cause any more bother.

Shuffling towards her, eyes still blurry from the flash of light, I stubbed my toe on the bedside table, had to stifle my 'Oyah!' sitting heavily on the bed. After I'd fiddled with the baby monitor, I stroked the hair back from her forehead. Like the way she used to when I was wee and ill. It was nice to see the tension away from her face, the pain gone. She looked younger. Well again, almost.

As she'd slept through the earlier racket I was hoping she'd make it to a decent hour without waking up. It worried me though when I was that tired. Sometimes it'd be fine and I'd hear her voice straight away, crackling with fear over the monitor, calling for Dad. Other times it would take a while for me to wake up. I'd only know she needed me when my dreams turned bad. Like I was on this big weird wooden boat and Dad was somewhere below decks but there's a storm at sea and Mum's out there in the waves, trying to swim but drowning slowly and I have to decide who I'm saving and when my hand grips the rail, I wake up.

I yawned wide enough for my jaw to crack. At least there hadn't been the usual tears. A moan about Colin's job prospects, her going on about having a brandy and me telling her no but other than that –

ZZZZZZZZOOOOOOOOOMMMM!

'*Fuck—!*' I nearly threw myself to the floor and the jolt woke her up, eyes flickering. 'Cathy? Is that... was that, was it thunder or something...? And were you...were you *swearing?*'

'No, no Mum, you're fine, we're fine, it's nothing. One of those ...' and I censored myself, '...one of those *tubes*. See? This is what I was talking about. About us moving to a lower flat, because that way like the O.T. was saying, you'd be able to get out more easily plus we wouldn't have these flying *numpties*...' but she wasn't listening. Tutting, working her head against the pillow, getting comfy, eyes closing against my rant. A minute or so later she was snoring softly again.

I was right though. It *was* dangerous up there, not just because she could have a fall going down the stairs. There'd been an article in the *Scotsman* about police helicopters getting fitted with breathalysers, superheroes having a few drams before they put their capes on. Just because they'd got superpowers, didn't stop them being Scottish. But there was no telling Mum. She'd get sentimental and go on about the view of the Tay, how elegant the rail bridge was, Tayport misty in the distance. How she and Dad bought this place for the sunsets. Not that Dad was here to see them now. Wherever he was.

Anyway.

I leant over, gave her a kiss goodnight. Not a murmur. Dead to the world and the second I thought the 'd-word', I wished that I hadn't.

I should have got straight to bed knowing the next day at work was going to be hellish in the aftermath of the nonsense outside. But walking past the ladder to the attic, I stopped. Although I didn't want to admit it, didn't want to give those lunatics the satisfaction, part of me wanted to see what was going on. It was like when you're sitting at home and hear fireworks going off somewhere in the city. You *know* they're miles away and you won't see anything but you end up standing at the window, staring at impossible angles, trying to get a view.

What put me off was it was *stupidly* late and up there was my old room. Kept like a shrine up there. As if I'd died. Still, I told myself, I could have a look around, decide what I was going to chuck. I was nearly thirty and there was loads of junk I should have got rid of years ago. I'd been meaning to do it since I moved back but what with Mum and work and everything, I hadn't had the chance. Five, ten minutes I'd give it.

The Studio I used to call it, pretentious wee git I was, though in my defence I *was* an art student. Used to spend hours up there, Mum passing meals up, nipping down to the toilet when I thought the coast was clear. There was room enough for a small bookcase made by me and Dad out of some planks from a skip, an old fashioned school desk (the hassle we had getting that up there), and a plastic chair that was too big for it. Every other square inch stuffed with piles of comics and sketchbooks covering the rug I'd made out of squares of carpet taped together from a book of samples Dad had got. The walls covered in pictures, cartoons and comic book covers mostly, some old movie stars – Marlene, Marilyn, Liz Taylor.

I went to switch the bare bulb on but realised the light of the moon was enough, clear and bright, giving everything a silvery glow. It felt like being stuck inside the head of a fourteen-year-old baby dyke but I surprised myself by liking it. It felt cosy. I could understand why I'd spent so much time up there.

The moon and the other lights. The weird ones, the supernatural glow of those show-offs. Which is when it clicked. A full moon. *That's* why they were at it, waking up the locals.

Ish had told me about it once in the pub after I'd started winding her up, slagging the Heroes. 'I mean, bridges. What is it with you superhero types and *bridges*. Is it some tourist attraction thing? And why every month? Is it like, hormonal? Like periods or something?'

She hadn't risen to it, hadn't used her powers to blow my eardrums out like any normal superhero would have done when dealing with her drunken girlfriend (not ex. Not then). Instead she'd given me this *you wouldn't understand* look which was only just starting to wind me up. She'd gone to speak then shrugged. 'I don't know. None of us know. It's stronger in some than in others and it just sort of ... happens. Y'know?' I nodded, even though of *course* I didn't know, what with me being Normal. 'Whenever there's a full moon we feel the pull. It's like ... pigeons.'

'Pigeons? What...like, *were*-pigeons?' I snorted and we laughed, the tension easing.

'Yeah, okay, maybe that's a bad example but you know how no one's sure how pigeons find their way when they're flying...' And it was my turn to give her a look. 'So I'm not explaining it very well but it's -'

'Big bloody pigeons,' I'd said, taking a gulp of my pint. '*Dangerous* pigeons with laser eyes and killer breath,' and that was the tension back again. Well done me. Like some toxic superpower. The gift of ruining a decent evening.

Ish. It had been a while since I'd seen her and I wondered if she was out there. I listened carefully, tried to make out from the warped 'Whumphs' and 'Krraaackkks' if there was singing going on. Ish's song, the Silver Selkie letting rip.

Not that I was fussed if she was there or not. None of my business what she got up to. If she wanted to hang about with a load of guys in dodgy spandex under bridges, that was up to her. Got her new friends to play with.

A dark blue light started to fill the room like water rising up past the window and I knew what that meant, who'd arrived to join the party. I craned my neck to see the moon turn blue with the white Saltire across it. What was *really* annoying was my heart started beating faster. I was as much a sucker for celebrity as anyone else.

The Fantoosh, the Phantom Fantoosh, greatest Scotsman ever born, out there strutting his stuff. Imagine a cross between a young Sean Connery and a Billy Connolly who can fly and lift really heavy stuff. Expressing so much charisma one flash of a smile would see a thousand Grannies swoon.

Flash git.

I was determined not to look, not turn into another fan-girl. I sat down at my desk instead, flicked through the notebook lying on top until I came to the drawing.

A man, a superhero with kiss-curl in place, cape flapping behind, one arm stretched out in front to ease him through the air, the skyscrapers surrounding him, 'CAPTAIN FANTASTIC!' in careful capitals arched above him. And I wondered if I realised the resemblance at the time. How much he looked like my Dad.

I must have been, what, fifteen when I drew it? Thinking I had a dazzling career as a comic book artist stretching ahead of me. Hah. What if I'd known the truth, what was going to happen ten years later? That when the great leap forward in humanity took place on my front doorstep, superheroes sprouting everywhere, I'd be working as a bloody civil servant, clearing up the mess. Probably chucked myself out of the attic window.

I traced a finger round Captain Fantastic's jaw-line, trying to keep the bitterness at bay. Maybe I knew back then what was going to happen to Dad and this was me trying to keep a hold of him. Something to remember him by, before he disappeared.

No. Didn't disappear. Was taken. By Kannyman, that mad bastard or superbeing or multidimensional whatever-the-fuck he/she/it *is*, who'd taken my Dad along with twenty-nine other Scots. Shortly after that came the Change, Superheroes popping up all over the place, then the folk with Abilities and *Christ*, I wanted my Dad back. Everything back to normal because normal was *good*.

I slammed the book shut, told myself it was the dust causing my eyes to prickle. I tapped the top of the desk then remembered what might be hidden there. Creaked up the lid and ... result! Still there, left from the last time I was up, was a half-empty packet of Marlboros and a quarter bottle of vodka, so cheap the label read only 'Vodka'.

'Faaantastic!' and I looked up out the window to see the Fantoosh surrounded by his blue and white shimmery glow flying low along the top of the Rail Bridge. As he passed a shower of glittering purple sparks fell from him, lighting the length of the bridge, the colour of thistles and heather falling into the river. Naturally because the Fantoosh took this whole being Scottish business *very* seriously. His sponsors would be disappointed if he didn't get his colour-scheme right.

I hated to admit it but it did look impressive. Breath-taking even. Put those poncy Edinburgh Festival Fireworks to shame. Aye, bonny Dundee, yah bas!

I pulled open the window and moved the desk back to sit on the top of it, elbows leaning on the sill. The fag was dry, crackled when I lit it, wouldn't last two minutes but it had been such a long night, the hit of it was bloody wonderful.

I took a swig of the vodka, gasping as I gulped. A few years back there'd have been crowds gathering to watch a spectacle like this, the police involved, keeping people back. Now it was random insomniacs like me and some die-hard fans braving the cold to stand by the Tay, cheering on their favourite, hoping for a photo or an autograph.

I did feel some of it that night though. The old magic, when the Change was starting to happen, miracles reported every half hour. I got a shiver up my spine and it wasn't just the cold. Maybe it was the nicotine, maybe the vodka, but the sweep of the bridge, that massive blue moon electrifying everything, giving the water a satiny look ... it got to me. And I felt like that fourteen year old again, in thrall to superpowers.

There were figures caped and in skin-tight suits swooping and dancing around the bridge's struts, playing chicken with a train (there'd be complaints about that), strange electrical charges causing the rails to glow orange, concrete seeming to bend and flow, twisting out into curling decorations. Mini-typhoons burst up from the water, dark coloured rainbows rose and vanished. That'd be the Northern Lights, the Cauld Blast causing the blizzard blanking some of the bridge from view, while the blazing horse, the Kelpie, with its flaming mane rode the waves under it, over to Tayport with that idiot, the Golden Eagle swooping down too close, nearly getting his wings singed, feathers skimming the surface of the water to cool them.

And all the while, looping the loop above them, the Phantom Fantoosh was leaving a trail of blue and white behind him, making Paisley patterns in the air, and his turns were so graceful, it was hypnotic watching and I forgot how sometimes on the TV he could come across as a bit of a sleazy chancer, with his day-old stubble and his floppy quiff. Here, he was like some kind of King.

I was starting to get it. Starting to get the point of the whole Flighting business. Since the Change, the *first* Change when the Superheroes appeared, most of them have gone corporate. Opening supermarkets, endorsing healthy eating, promoting Scottish tourism. Well, wasn't as if the country was overrun with supervillains, was it? Here they were enjoying the chance to let their hair down. Let rip. The equivalent of the rest of us, the Normals, getting wasted on a Friday night. I was almost feeling sympathetic, a wee tear in my eye as the fireballs and snowballs and – what was that? ectoplasm? – flew about when I heard it.

No, not it. Ish.

Her song started as a drone, so low I wasn't sure if it was there or not, had to tilt my head to catch it. Then it snagged my ear and poured in, filling me up with an ache, a sweet, sad tone calling me, seeping into my soul, making it thrum and I knew I didn't deserve to hear it, it was too beautiful, too much. Like Liz Fraser and Jeff Buckley and Billie Holiday and Billy MacKenzie combined, too good and pure for the likes of me.

It was Ish but not *my* Ish. Not any more. She'd become the Silver Selkie and she'd set the bridge singing, ringing out in perfect pitch, turning it into one giant instrument. Some of the music was like a celebration but some of it was full of sadness too. It was like she was saying, singing out full-throated, 'Hey! You! All you miserable Normal folk, come and look! Isn't this *amazing*! Isn't it *incredible*! And it's awful and *cruel* that you can only watch and we get to *do* this stuff! And how, can somebody please tell me *why*, did everything get so beautifully, so wonderfully, so very fucked up!'

I listened a few minutes more until I'd had enough, couldn't bear it and slammed the window shut against the chill and Ish's song. Listened instead for my Mum crying in the dark.

The Burry Man by Diana Hope

CONTRIBUTORS

Peter Burnett is the author of Scotland or No, #freetopiary: An Occupy Romance, The Studio Game, The Supper Book and other titles.

Ken Crump was a founding editor of the Pacific Northwest literary magazine The Duckabush Journal. He has published various chapbooks, including Last of the Bohemian Kings. In 1992 Ken moved permanently to Edinburgh.

Elizabeth Darling is Reader in Architectural History at Oxford Brookes University. The Society of Antiquaries of Scotland helped to fund the research which underpins this article.

Lou Dear enjoys teaching seminars on literature, ideology and identity at the University of Glasgow and training – with enthusiasm and not distinction – at United Glasgow, an anti-racist football team.

Robert Davies is from South Wales. He completed his Masters in Design in Photography at Glasgow School of Art and currently works at Edinburgh College of Art.

Lucy Ellmann is a novelist because no one has ever allowed her to work in a shop.

Eddie Gibbons is an economic migrant from 1980s Liverpool. He recently retired from a career in clock watching and watch clocking in order to spend more time with his biro and his Giro, and to work on that all-important seventh poetry collection.

Jim Gilchrist is a freelance writer, for many years a staff journalist with The Scotsman, for which he still writes a music (folk/jazz) column.

Joyce Guthrie worries about Edinburgh as if it was one of her children. She walks the city in the early morning and at night fills her wastepaper basket to the brim.

Diana Hope trained at Edinburgh College of Art and exhibits throughout Scotland, most recently at An Talla Sollas in Ullapool.

Tom Hubbard was the first Librarian of the Scottish Poetry Library, from 1984 to 1993, before leaving to take lecturing posts in the United States, France and Hungary, which were followed by visiting professorships in the same countries. He is the author, editor or co-editor of over thirty academic and literary works.

James Kelman, author of drama, fiction and non-fiction, lives in Glasgow, Scotland.

Brian McLaughlin has lived and taught in the U.S.A., France, India and Catalonia. A graduate of University of Edinburgh, his doctoral thesis in literature centred on the construction of identity.

Ali Millar lives and works in Edinburgh where she studied MA Creative Writing at Napier University and graduated with the class medal. The founder of the website Bear Got Books, she is working on her first novel.

Kenny Munro is a graduate of Edinburgh College of Art and The Royal College of Art London, a former chairman of Edinburgh Sculpture workshop and a director of Sir Patrick Geddes Memorial Trust.

Petra Reid is a poet artist whose proper job as a welfare rights adviser informs her practice.

Kirsti Wishart's stories have appeared in New Writing Scotland, The One O'Clock Gun Anthology and The Seven Wonders of Scotland. In 2013 she was awarded a Hawthornden Writing Fellowship. The novel she's currently working on features a remote island, knitting, codes and lots of sheep.

David Wheatley is the author of several books of poetry, including A Nest on the Waves (Gallery Press).

Neil Young hails from Belfast and now lives in Stonehaven. His first collection, Lagan Voices, was published by Scryfa in 2009. A booklet of sonnets, The Parting Glass, is due out from Tapsalteerie in December.